The Second Arrow

Guilt After Suicide Loss
A Memoir

Roberta Halpern

"Losing someone you love is the first arrow. You feel acute pain of loss and sorrow. But worrying, being anxious, or succumbing to despair are like the second arrow…Our guilt, remorse, and regrets are the second arrow we often fire at ourselves."

—Thich Nhat Hanh

This book is dedicated to all who have felt there was more they could have done for a loved one they lost. May you find peace.

In the end, my daughter wrote that she hated me and I believed her.

Contents

PROLOGUE

Two Suitcases

September 1, 2017

I feel weird—like an alien who has arrived from a distant planet. My daughter has killed herself and I must be responsible in some way. Either I caused it or I didn't prevent it, and now everyone is looking at me and they must know that I am guilty.

At Denver Airport I have two suitcases. In my carry-on bag, there is a navy blue cardboard box in a navy blue cloth bag which holds the ashes of my daughter Suzanne. This container sits in the space that I had left for it when I flew into Denver to clean out her apartment just four days after her death at at age 37. I also have a certificate from the Apollo Funeral Home acknowledging that in the box are the remains of my daughter in ash form.

My womb held my daughter for nine months. When she entered the world, she rested in my arms. She has been transported by baby pack, car seat, and bicycle seat when she was young and breathing. But, carting around the remains of my child is not normal–it is not something any mother in human form should be doing.

The checked bag is Suzanne's. In it I placed her important paperwork, her two journals, her phone and computer. My gut told me these needed to be with me. The detective noted that one of the journals contained the "suicide note," which I will get to study later. For now, I can see that my daughter was angry and that she hated me when she left. And my brain cannot process any of that now. My brain does not want to.

Also in the checked bag are make-up brushes, jewelry, two SEPTA tokens, a lime green measuring teaspoon, and a dragonfly dish—items which I hope to use and save as remembrances of my daughter, not that I will ever forget her.

At Denver International Airport, it is all serious business. I don't see a trace of humanity in the face of the security guard insisting on scanning the navy blue box for drugs.

It is strange and ironic and I wonder if the drugs that Suzanne injected into her veins from a drip bag hung from her bedroom wall, the drugs that took away her breath and her life almost instantly, will be identifiable in the remains. Will the surface of the box still have any residue? As an alien, I do not know these things.

The agent finds no drugs, but I wonder if you think it strange that I should have these thoughts. I don't know what grief looks like on my face or how I can move my body just one week after my daughter's death as I make my way home to Philadelphia. My body puts one foot down and then the other without effort or awareness, dragging behind it the suitcase that houses Suzanne's ashes in between my blouses and my beige and army-green capri pants.

Is it possible that I look awful or scared or in shock? What does shock look like on a face?

There is a photo taken of my brother and me from late November, 2000, just six weeks after my younger daughter Lisa died at age 18. My brother is wearing a festive jester type hat in red and green, while my face is pale and worn and wan. Every muscle is sad and droopy and long even though I am trying to smile. It is as though sadness had woven its way into my skin by way of my cells, by way of my broken heart.

I guess I look similarly in the Denver airport. It is still so fresh and new. Shock had enabled me to do the work that needed to be done in the apartment, with the help of a couple of Suzanne's friends. Now that is done and I'm not sure how my face looks.

It appears that these guards are trained to look for signs of weird and/or dangerous behaviors and unusual signs of distress such as a suicide bomber might exhibit, and maybe he is sensing something weird about me.

When they test the box of Suzanne's ashes and everything is good, I am relieved. At least I'm not a drug smuggler. Perhaps the agent with the serious face is wondering what's up with me. Or not.

Maybe the search is random and he doesn't give a darn about what anybody is thinking or feeling. Maybe the newness of this grief makes my face appear normal. Maybe it has not yet morphed into the dripping face of sadness. Maybe focusing on everyone else prevents me from the depth of feelings that must eventually emerge.

Thankfully, there's a restaurant near my gate where I can store my luggage. It is so easy to slide the carry-on bag under the table designed for this purpose. Easy has not been a word in my vocabulary this week, so I am grateful and almost ecstatic when I discover this table feature. In addition, the waiter sees me as human and somehow I manage to order beer and food and enjoy this temporary time where no one knows about me or my alien origins. The word *enjoy* here is relative. I am no longer a drug smuggling suspect, so I can relax for the moment. Relief feels a little bit like joy. The server doesn't know how I am feeling or what I am going through. I am safe in my anonymity. For the time being, I put the reality of my situation aside, so my body can consume some nourishment. Although most of the meal is not memorable, the tricolored potatoes are. I mean, how often do you see white, purple, and orange potatoes all on the same plate?

Afterward, I find my way to the gate seating area and prepare to do a little writing. Before I settle in with my journal, I call an ex-boyfriend, Vincent, who had gotten to know Suzanne pretty well. Almost immediately I know this has been a mistake. He rambles on and on about his current girlfriend and his broken air conditioner, but I am from the planet that does not understand and cannot hear or respond to such mundane things. I cannot get off the phone fast enough.

One Week Earlier

Aug. 25, 2017

"I'm sick of this shit!" The words just spill out of my mouth at the 12-step meeting. This statement refers to the frustration I feel about not being able to help my adult daughter, who has been in relapse mode for three years, after 11 years of sobriety.

I'm a mess and desperate for some support. There's Al-Anon in Philly for friends and families of alcoholics, but not the specialized Parent's Group that helped me so much when I lived in Manhattan. So, on a steamy late August day, I take the grueling two-hour Bolt Bus ride from Philly to NYC, then the C train from Penn Station to the Upper West Side.

This is a gentle program and I am not new to Al-Anon. Also, this is not Suzanne's first relapse, but it will be her last. Some of the other parents look at me with understanding eyes. My presence in these rooms goes back to the 90's when dealing with the ex-husband. But it has been a while since I've been to a meeting and I am not feeling very gentle.

The people in this room know what it's like to have a child of any age struggle with the disease of addiction. A few are taken aback with my bluntness. But I am venting—I'm sick of the relapses, sick of the ups and downs over the years, sick of having to go to meetings. I'm just sick of the whole thing.

There's another reason I make the trip into New York for this very special parents' meeting. In the last two weeks there's been a shift in our relationship. Suzanne is angry with me. This is not new. Anger has popped up from time to time over the years when memories and realizations come back to her. As her imperfect mother, I accept those moments, listen as best I can, and apologize as many times as needed for whatever happened that cannot now be changed.

This time is different. When old anger surfaces, she doesn't want to hear any apologies. She *needs space,* she tells me. She also tells me she *feels like hurting me,* so I shouldn't visit. I have never heard her say that before and I am surprised and concerned. I respect her wishes and tell her to take all the time she needs.

I have a plane ticket to Denver for the first weekend of September, which I don't cancel, even though she tells me not to come. She is 37, an adult, living 1700 miles away. She has great friends and is working with a therapist. I do my best to convince myself that she will be okay.

But, as she is creating distance from me, she is doing the same with most of her closest friends, And none of us knows she is pulling away from all of us.

And on that day, while I am expressing my frustration at the meeting, Suzanne is already gone.

PART I

Before

The Name

A child was conceived in love. There was love—I'm sure of it. And the couple was excited to bring new life into the world. Because they shared a love for romance—words and music, literature and poetry, it made sense they chose the name they did.

If it was a girl it would be Suzanne, inspired by the Leonard Cohen, song, although they preferred the Judy Collins version. The Suzanne of the song is resourceful, captivating, a little crazy, a little magical. They saw their daughter's future with the name. There was both a haunting and spiritual quality to the song. And a purity of love and acceptance.

What if it was a boy? Michael. That was it. No special significance to choosing that name-just a nice name that the couple liked.

Maybe they always knew their first child would be a girl.

CHAPTER 1

In Utero-1979

We are married two years, when I find out I'm pregnant. Our plan was for me to teach five years but it's a year shy. For my 25th birthday, just a year before, I had stopped smoking, already thinking of a healthy start for a baby.

I attend weekly ballet classes in my shiny navy blue Danskin leotard with a pink ballet skirt, pink tights, and pink Capezio pointe shoes. My obstetrician gives me permission to dance *en pointe* until the 6th month. There are pliés at the barre, adagios and perfectly balanced pirouettes in the center. I am in prime shape and love the dance. My unborn child and I share the rhythmic movements and classical music.

In excellent health, with no morning sickness, I become the poster child for pregnancy. That mysterious radiant glow that everyone talks about a pregnant woman having? I've got it. My energy is electric—filled with excitement for who will soon be here for loving and cuddling. My face beams and my heart softens and deepens. Other people around me notice this and strangers strike up conversations.

We agree that I will leave teaching at the end of the year, in my fifth month. Staying home with my children for several years is part of the plan we made before we married.

Reading everything I can about natural childbirth and breast feeding becomes my passion. What interests me especially is the Lamazze breathing technique, which is based on the idea that tension causes pain, a revelation to me, yet so simple. By relaxing with deep breathing, you can eliminate some of the pain of childbirth. I give up alcohol, take my pre-natal vitamins, and eat healthy, fully confident that I am doing everything right to begin this new relationship with my unborn child.

One evening at summer's end, I am outstretched on the bed, in my lightweight pink kimono, propped up on a pile of pillows, a fan blowing cool air on me. My waist-length hair is pulled up in a ballet bun, because of that darn Long Island humidity. With a book in my hands that I am studying intently, something about childbirth, there is nothing but hope and optimism about what the future holds.

I make a silent vow to do everything possible I can for my child, who I am totally in love with already, but don't yet know will be a girl.

My husband saunters into the room holding his second or third Black Russian. I sit up straight There is something on his mind. He seems nervous and agitated. He paces on the side of the room. I place the book down on my lap carefully so as not to lose the page.

He has decided to ask for my opinion on something we have not discussed in our two years of dating and our two years of marriage. And now I am seven months pregnant and jobless.

He remains standing, almost hovering, while I am still on the bed. I listen until he finishes. It doesn't take much thought to know how I feel, so I decide to simply be truthful. This is not what he wants to hear.

Next thing I know a glass zooms past my head and into the wall, where it makes an indentation. Black liquid drips down the wall where it begins to puddle on the floor.

Tension fills my body, I can't move—I am now frozen. I do not fight back. I do not run. There is silence. Lots of thick heavy lengthy silence. Who is this person I married?

At some point, I remember to breathe. Yes, I have just read about that. Tension causes pain. What just happened does not compute. I keep breathing. My fear produces adrenaline and cortisol. I imagine these chemicals making their way directly to my unborn child by way of the umbilical cord that connects us. These are not the lovely gentle feelings produced in ballet class. Good thing I am sitting down, because standing up, I would be unbalanced, feeling faint, and nauseous.

Seven months pregnant, no job and, no one to tell about this, I register an instantaneous decision.

My being decides then, in the midst of chaos, confusion, and fear, to shut down a part of itself, because this will be the best way to survive this marriage. In that moment no other options exist.

CHAPTER 2

Early Years

Suzanne and I begin to bond with on-demand nursing. Throughout day and night, we cuddle on the rocking chair. Sometimes at the dinner table. Sometimes I sing to her. Always, I tell her how beautiful and special she is and how much I love her Such a precious time between us which lasts nine months, when she becomes bored with the breast and more interested in the world beyond. She covets the cup and wants whatever I have in it, and so it comes to be. No more breast.

By the time Suzanne's a toddler we can't wait for her father to arrive home from school. We share a car and as a stay-at-home mom, I look forward to getting out of the house to buy a loaf of bread or a gallon of milk. Our favorite outing is the library where we always return with a big stack of children's books. Reading has replaced nursing for our bonding time. Suzanne loves nursery rhymes and picture books. We read them over and over, so much so that she begins to memorize them. She fills in the ending of rhyming lines and quotes passages from books in unexpected moments.

At a family Easter dinner, when the behind-scheduled coq au vin finally arrives, everyone is quiet except Suzanne. "That meal was worth waiting for!" she announces to laughter all around. At a relative's barbeque, my precocious daughter tells everyone she meets. "It was a pleasure to have met you." Both statements come directly from library books.

For me, the library becomes a refuge, a place to find community and culture. For Suzanne, besides books, there are puzzles and games, and children's programs, like the Magical Musical Storyteller. Suzanne is mesmerized by her glittery costume and her lilting tales. She never wants to leave.

One day she has so much fun, that when it's time to go, she lays on the floor, screaming and crying—sobbing and wailing, because she doesn't want to leave the library.

I get it. Neither do I.

Two years and two months after Suzanne, Lisa is born. As they grow, they become best friends. When the kids are little everyone comes to visit us, but when they are no longer babies, I take them on Sundays to visit my mom, Grandma Lila, In Queens, New York. Now I have my own vehicle, a white station wagon which I purchased with a loan from my in-laws. The girls and I look forward to this adventure, while my husband is happy to remain home. As the marriage sours, we all get a little break from the tension in the house.

As we speed along the Long Island Expressway, windows open, our hair blowing, we sing at the top of our lungs. With melodies on our lips we forget the troubles at home. Practicing some rounds of "Row Row Row Your Boat," and "Frere Jaques," we mess up, of course, laugh about it, and begin again. As they get older, we sing songs they learn in school. I share songs from my days as a Girl Scout. *Make New Friends, but keep the old, One is silver and the other gold. Kookaburra sits in the old oak tree, merry merry king of the bush is he*....Singing in the car becomes our thing, a Mom and the girls' thing.

Grandma lives at the top of a steep staircase on the second floor of a garden apartment in Little Neck. It is part of the city, but feels a little closer to suburbia, with its quiet streets, strip malls, and no close access to a subway. The girls love going there, because my mother loves to spoil them with gifts, and affection, and special treats. She makes potato pancakes for Chanukah and does Passover and Rosh Hashanah dinners. My husband comes to the special days but avoids the Sunday visits.

On Sundays, the girls get all the attention. There is always a tasty lunch with bagels and cream cheese and lox, tuna fish, and egg salad. Nothing fancy, but it feels special. And of course, lots of sweets—candy and cookies and soda. The love from Grandma is unconditional and large. It is a safe haven for all of us.

And there's more singing in the car going home. I share songs I learned from summer camp where counselors would strum their guitars and sing folk songs of the 60's. I pass them along to my girls. Now we are all singing them."If I had a Hammer" and "Michael Row Your Boat Ashore." Hallelujah.

By the time Suzanne enters kindergarten, I begin to observe her deep sensitivity. One day she arrives home from school sullen and sad. Her face is long and she won't tell me what's wrong. I keep at it and eventually, the long face convulses into a sobbing mess. She can barely get the words out, " I... I .. threw out the plum." It takes her a minute to recover from the sobs. She glances up with one eye to see how I react. I am relieved that this is all it is. I'm not sure if she is sad for the plum, or for me, who has given it to her for her snack. Or maybe, it's about throwing out food. All I know is she cares deeply about this. Very deeply. I take her into my arms. "Don't worry, honey," I say. "It's all right." She stays there for a while and we breathe.

She was around the same age when we take her to see the movie *ET* in the theaters. She cries for three whole days afterward.

CHAPTER 3

Sick House

Years pass.

From the outside, the house on Carrie Avenue appears normal. Better than normal, even. Lawns are mowed and perennials and flowering bushes bloom at various stages of the seasons for optimum color effect. There are annuals planted in the front and a vegetable garden in the back that produces an abundance of healthy crops. Those who pass by admire how lovely the house looks.

"Don't ever let that man go," a friend comments to the woman one day, in reference to how nice the house was kept.

But inside is different. The house keeps secrets, even though moments of peace, joy, and laughter often squeeze through the cracks. There is a sickness, a tension in the family that the house holds onto. Because the man carries his anger and the woman retains that shutdown part, a wound grows in the marriage. And neither of them knows how to talk about it. So they don't. It festers and blisters and becomes infected.

Mostly they just try to look and act normal, and do normal things, for appearances, in the way that the house looks beautiful on the outside. There are moments and times they fool everyone with their exterior normalcy, by pretending the rift between them does not exist. But the sickness worsens and becomes an ugly gangrenous sore in need of amputation.

The house keeps all the secrets—the drinking and the ugly fights between the man and the woman. It keeps the night terrors and the bedwetting of the children. The secret self-mutilating of the older daughter.

The woman has no friends or family to confide in. Neither does the man. The children in the house see everything. And hear everything. And feel everything. They see what they see and they feel what they feel and even if they don't have words or aren't given words for their experiences, their bodies respond to the thick, murky, veiled tension that exists between their parents. The house expands and swells with the tension. The tension becomes a monster that swallows up the living space and the air until everyone is gasping. Even the dog feels it and develops a skin condition, that never goes away.

One day the younger child takes a social studies text book and throws it at her window breaking the glass, just to relieve the pressure... for the moment.

CHAPTER 4

Tears in Heaven, 1991

"Suzanne's trying to throw up!" Lisa, now 10, is shouting from the bathroom. Like every morning, getting the kids off to school is my responsibility, while my husband has already left for work. This is Friday and the weekend of my middle school's musical production. As the director/producer, my head buzzes with all the tasks needed to make the three sold-out performances happen. Could it be that my 12-year-old daughter has an eating disorder? Really? Now? I don't have time for this. Recently she has been overly interested in counting her calories.

I open the door.

Lisa is not finished. Now she is shouting, "Suzanne took aspirin. Suzanne took aspirin!!" There is an open bottle on the counter. Suzanne has told Lisa that she has taken 27 aspirin. Now I am screaming, "Why did you do that? What were you thinking?" Suzanne's eyes are filled with regret. The screaming is not helping.

I don't think. I yell for them both to get in the car and we head for the closest hospital, which is in Patchogue, the next big town. Lisa has not stopped screaming. Suzanne sits is in the front seat and doesn't appear to be sick in any way. She is quiet and offers no information. Lisa continues to yell, "You are so stupid. Why did you do that?" over and over. She is pissed. I've got one kid who feels everything deeply, taking it all in on herself, and one kid who gets her anger out in full display for everyone.

In my panicked and frozen state, it's those blue and white H for Hospital road signs that guide me. Those signs are the breadcrumbs to safety, a way out of the dangerous and scary forest. I rejoice at seeing the next one. And the next. Although it is my body seated behind the steering wheel, an ancient part of my survival brain is finding its way to the hospital and I am getting closer to the emergency room with my daughter who has tried to kill herself with aspirin. And although I am sick to my stomach, I am also so in love with the creator of those blue hospital signs.

When my daughter is safely admitted, my thoughts return to the performances, which must go on. I am forced to compartmentalize and focus on necessary tasks. During the performances, I am to sit with the script and communicate by headphones with the stage and lighting crews. We have been rehearsing for months, including nights, weekends, and vacations. Everyone depends on me. I will have to show up and try to pretend I'm not dying on the inside.

At the hospital, my husband takes the Friday night shift, as Suzanne gets charcoal to deactivate the effects of the aspirin and a psychiatrist talks with her. *She is alive. She is alive.* I say those words in my head over and over. I turn on the radio in the car as I drive to visit her. Eric Clapton's "Tears in Heaven" comes on. It is about his young son, who falls from a window and dies. I can't listen to it without crying. But there is not much time now for my tears.

I manage to get through the weekend and the play goes well enough, although it's just a blur. Suzanne is discharged on Monday. The professionals are convinced that she won't harm herself again and they cite her good grades as an indicator that she's not that bad off. That's what I want to believe. But, I am petrified.

Suzanne's suicide attempt forces me to finally look at what is going on in my house, as much as I would rather escape from it with my obsessive working. The situation, I now know, has become so sick that it has become deadly. I don't quite know where to start.

So, I become hypervigilant. I think every action in the household will cause another suicide attempt. My husband interprets Suzanne's attempt as manipulative and he's angry, but I see it as a cry for help. Suzanne, I will realize, becomes the barometer for how things are faring in the family. And by the looks of Suzanne's behaviors, it's a mess, a deadly mess. And it is now right in my face and I can't look away.

About a week later, Suzanne gets up on a stage and sings a solo in her junior high choral concert. She sings clearly and beautifully. While I watch this performance, I look around at the packed house and wonder if everyone who *knows* is thinking what I am thinking—*how can she even sing after being through such an ordeal?* And I come to understand that music is her lifeline.

There are numerous attempts to get Suzanne into therapy, but she resists. Her junior high school counselor tells me that she is *the toughest nut to crack th*at she has ever seen. At one counseling session, she plugs herself into her Walkman, slumps low in the chair, and sinks into her inward place, tuning out the therapist. Eventually, she admits to me that she has also experimented by taking other kinds of poisons like little bits of detergent. She also reveals that has been cutting herself.

I know this is not good, not good at all. And I know that I don't know how to help her or the marriage or myself.

Everyone in the family tries counseling, but I am the only one who goes consistently. After a year, not much changes in the house. I live in fear of another suicide attempt and the anger of my husband. I can't keep living in the dysfunction so I ask my husband to leave. Without missing a beat, he tells me he is going to rehab.

At the rehab, there is "Family Weekend," and I am invited. I am angry that he gets to go to a beautiful facility on Chesapeake Bay, while I am left at home to pick up the pieces. It is not how I envisioned spending my 39th birthday, but I go.

It is the beginning of my education about the disease of addiction, a rebirth of sorts. On Saturday, the first day of Family Weekend, there's a "graduation" ceremony for one of the patients. He has to tell his story to a small group. The story is not exactly the same as ours, but close enough. He talks about the familiar chaos, the fights, and struggles, his regrets, and his willingness to start over fresh and sober. I begin to cry. All the tears that had been held back over the years just come down in rivers. It is the first time I realize I am not alone. I try to prevent myself from sobbing out loud. "Can I go home now?" is all I can say afterward.

But they are not done with me yet. The next day they bring an Al-Anon meeting to the facility and tell me I have to go. People had been telling me to go to Al-Anon for some time. Now I have no choice.

The people at the meeting. are smiling and laughing. *How could this be?* I wonder, *when there is so much serious trauma in their families?* I learn from people sharing their experience, strength, and hope, that I want what they have — a life — even amid pain. Like a good student, I follow directions and keep going to meetings when I get home.

We have a calm summer, but when the stresses of going back to work return, my husband relapses. By October, we are right back where we were before, even though I have a lot more knowledge thanks to the program. And again, Suzanne the barometer starts to fall, signaling a storm on the way.

One night in late October, while hanging out with some friends, she takes off running like a roadrunner, down the railroad tracks—the tracks where actual trains run. She completely freaks out her friends, who don't know if she is trying to kill herself again. She ends up in an emergency psych facility where she is released right away. Even though the professionals feel that this incident isn't enough for them to admit her, it is, however, enough for me to ask my husband to leave again—this time I mean business. And he leaves. And never comes back to the house.

Now I can focus on my children. That is my intention.

CHAPTER 5

Amputation

Part of the festering wound is removed, but the house does not heal right away. There is of course the phenomenon of the phantom wound, where unhealthiness and pain are still felt. The house continues to hold it, remember it, feel it. The energy begins to change and the dynamic shifts and everyone remaining in the house begins to bounce.

The inhabitants react to the removal of the arguments, the repression, and the fear. They go from one extreme to the other. The release from repression creates a freedom of sorts. Too much freedom results in anarchy. So that's what the house turns into for a while. There is still alcohol but now the older daughter begins to use it. To excess. As a young teenager.

The younger daughter follows whatever the older daughter does.

After some time, the woman starts dating an artist, who takes her to cultural events and late nights in NYC, and opens up her creative energy. This is beneficial to the woman in the long run. However, for the moment, it's at the *expense of the children who do not have proper supervision some of the time. So there are teenage parties and trouble. The woman will say that they were all teenagers together for a while. It seemed necessary to the process.*

The younger daughter, who always saw things more clearly, and would express her views succinctly with uncomplicated vocabulary, would say that her mother had gone away for a while but then came back. Simple.

One time after the daughters had a party while the woman was somewhere with the artist, all the screens in the outdoor porch end up torn beyond repair. They would need to be replaced. The daughters stand and study the woman, who is definitely not the father. "You're not going to hit us?" one of the daughters asks, her face looking perplexed. That is not the woman's style and she tells them. "I'm disappointed, but I'm not going to hit you." It made the woman wonder if the father had hit them frequently, because surely, she had not been witness to that. Or she couldn't remember. Or didn't want to.

The concept of discipline without physical punishment is apparently a novel idea to her daughters. The woman begins to realize that there is a lot to uncover that she has forgotten or perhaps had never known in the chaos of the sick house.

One afternoon the woman arrives home from teaching to find a note from the older daughter, "I'm at Alexis's house.

Don't call," which of course makes the woman want to call more than anything.

And when she does, she learns that Alexis has left her mother a note saying she is staying at a different friend's house. Hmmmm. The two mothers make a few more calls. None of the teenagers are where they are supposed to be. Where are they? The two mothers figure out that these teenagers have a grand plan, to all meet at Bay Road, the local teenage hangout. No good can come of that.

These mothers are smart, having been teenagers themselves. And they are going to mess up this plan big time. They contact as many parents as they can and arrange a party-crashing caravan with the woman leading the pack. Her teal Ford Escort's bright headlights blare into the eyes of the surprised teens gathering at Bay Road. The parents gleefully succeed in busting up the ruse before the party gets wild. The older daughter is silent and pouty when she is told to get in the car, and when she gets home, she slams the door of her room while yelling at her mother that she hates her.

Mom is back!

But that doesn't prevent things from getting even worse.

CHAPTER 6

Rehab Tour

The Bay Road incident was a nice save, but the kids don't give up. They get more creative. The drinking continues and so do the trips to the emergency room.

One freezing December day, just a couple of months after my husband leaves, Suzanne gets drunk with some friends after school. She arrives home early without her key and smashes her hand through the back window to break into the house. When I arrive home soon afterward, I see her wrist wrapped in a towel.

At the walk-in clinic, the doc gives her a couple of stitches and talks to her about drinking. To my surprise, he connects this act to alcoholism and explains that it is a chronic disease. "The only treatment is to not drink and go to meetings," he tells her. I applaud his honesty, but Suzanne isn't having any of it.

When we get home from the clinic, Suzanne settles in on the living room couch while I make dinner. Behind the couch, in front of our window is our Christmas tree, waiting to be decorated. This will be our first Christmas without my husband in the house. Since he was a Christian and I a Jew, he was always in charge in picking out the tree. And he had a system which involved counting the number of bottom branches.

I was going to do it my way. How hard could it be? So I made a quick decision and chose the first tree that looked to be about the right size. But this particular one kept wanting to lean. The leaning tower of tree. I had finagled something with shiny green curling ribbon and a ceiling plant hook, a temporary fix which I thought quite clever.

When I walk into the living room to check on Suzanne, she is passed out. The tree had loosened itself from the shiny ribbon and although braced by the arm of the couch, the upper portion of the evergreen was gently resting upon her, like a Christmas tree blanket. She has no idea and doesn't feel a thing. Luckily, the incident causes little damage and I can see the humor in the moment.

Suzanne is not drinking every day, but I notice that when she does drink, she gets drunk, deeply drunk. I try to talk to her when she is sober, telling her that this is not a good choice. And that she could make a different, healthier choice, considering the alcoholism in the family. I feel my words fall on deaf ears.

There is another time, when she and Alexis, her partner in crime, are found wandering the streets dodging traffic while drunk and brought to another emergency room. When I receive a phone call to take her home to sleep it off,

I realize how lucky we are that nothing worse happened. No injury. No arrest. No death. And I am grateful for the anonymous angels who help and protect them that day.

The most dramatic and severe of the incidents occurs when she goes off a friend's roof while drunk. I am called by the friend's family and find my way to the emergency room, where I can hear Suzanne screaming in pain as they stitch up her face. Her jaw is broken and it will be wired shut for some weeks. Alone in the waiting room, I pace back and forth, saying the Serenity Prayer that I have learned in Al-Anon.

God, Grant me the Serenity to

Accept the things I cannot change,

Courage to change the things I can,

And the Wisdom to know the difference.

From this low point begins a process that eventually gets her help. This time insurance authorities cannot be certain that she didn't jump, so they recommend a psychiatric facility. With the doctors' approval, I can get the necessary insurance coverage to pay for it.

And so begins what I call the Upstate Rehab Tour, when I drive Suzanne to and from different facilities that begin to address the issues that have been building for years.

First stop—Four Winds Psychiatric Facility in Westchester County, just north of Manhattan. I miss my first day of teaching, to drive Suzanne there. "Family first," my kind principal says, when I tell him what I need to do. After a couple of weeks, she comes home to her room freshly painted by my artist boyfriend, who covers the walls with a beautiful shade of lavender, Suzanne's favorite color. He cleans up all the graffiti that she and her friends had spray-painted during our lawless, anarchistic, teenage rebellion period. In truth, her room looked like a crack house. Because of the broken jaw, Ensure and other liquid foods are all she can eat. She loves the new room and the fresh start and we have a quiet week or two.

But her drug-user boyfriend shows up one day and is so kind as to provide her some heroin "for the pain," which I don't find out about until months later, when Suzanne approaches me. "Mom I need help." Hearing that my child is using heroin scares the shit out of me. Alcohol is familiar. Alcohol I knew. It wasn't good, but heroin? That is a whole other level. And wrapping my brain around that isn't easy.

How can my brilliant and talented daughter be using heroin? How did I let this happen? Flashing through my brain are images of down and out people living in the streets with needles in their arms.

But none of those thoughts help. I need to take action.

So I take her back to Four Winds, because this is all I know at the time. There she detoxes. Then they tell me she now needs a drug rehab.

Stop 2 is Arms Acres, a drug rehab further upstate. She stays a month. But the drug dealer boyfriend is still lurking around at home, waiting to pounce. A wise counselor says that if Suzanne is in a good place, she will slam the door or the window on the drug-user boyfriend, if he comes a-knocking. But, she isn't in that place at all—she isn't even close. I can tell by her body language—her slump in the chair, her head hanging low on "graduation" day, that she is just biding time to get back home.

So I have to figure out the next step. She can't come home. It is too risky. And now I am thinking about Lisa and trying to keep her safe from drugs and alcohol too. My boyfriend, who lives about 30 miles away, volunteers to take her in, so she can enroll in a different school district and have a fresh start. She will be far enough away from my place, so her boyfriend won't be able to find her.

I tell myself that we are having an underground resistance movement, a white market, for good. Everything starts great with my boyfriend, but he hasn't thought through the challenges of living with a young rebellious teenager, who even though she is sober, doesn't want to live by the rules. After a couple of months of mutual admiration, school is out for the summer and these two begin to get on each other's nerves. The honeymoon is over and they begin having arguments. He works some nights and is not as available to supervise her. Suzanne's anger comes out and so does my boyfriend's. So this situation needs to end.

We are running out of ideas.

CHAPTER 7

The Family Foundation School, 1995

I thought I had exhausted all my options when I put my 15-year-old daughter on the street. Technically, it was a parking lot in a strip mall in an affluent, safe town about 30 minutes away. It was a lovely summer night and she would be going to a friend's house, just a short walk away, but it felt like I was putting her on the street. I didn't know what else to do.

Having tried every avenue of possibility—psychiatric facility, drug rehab, even hiding her at my boyfriend's house in a different town, to keep her from the drug addict boyfriend, I had come up empty.

So, I decide, with the help of my support group, that she can't come back home. I need to protect Lisa. Although Suzanne is sober at the moment, her behaviors are out of control, and proximity to the old drug friends, especially the boyfriend, is not advantageous.

During this time, there is not a lot of communication between us. She had asked for help and that's how she ended up in the rehab, but these programs are short and I feel like there needs to be more time for her, for all of us, to recover from all the years of trauma in the family.

As a single parent now for a couple years, it's all up to me. And I don't have much breathing room. There is no time to process the ending of the marriage. I simply respond to the next event as it occurs.

I don't sleep much that night and hope she is okay. It is difficult to accept that I have no control over the situation. In Al-Anon, they have a slogan, *Let Go and Let God*, God being some higher power that is not you. That's what I am doing here. I pray a lot, because it's the only thing I have left. It has gone out of my hand's into the hands of the Universe.

***

The next day the doorbell rings. I'm in the kitchen when I hear a groan from Lisa, who is sprawled out on the living room couch watching TV. "Oh noooo… *she's* back."

Suzanne is standing on the stoop, peering through the glass door looking sheepish and forlorn. With her is a friend who she has met at an AA meeting. "I want to tell you about this school," she says. I don't open the door. I am angry and frustrated and don't want to hear anything.

"I want to tell you about this school," she persists. There is something in her tone and manner that inspires me to open the door. I let them in and we sit around the kitchen table. I listen while she and the friend explain that there is a school upstate based on the 12 Steps. He had gone there and it turned his life around. And now Suzanne wants to go there. She is asking for help—again.

I am skeptical of everything, having seen that she didn't appear to benefit from the help offered to her in the past. But, she seems to think this might work. Since she has found the option, I think there may be a chance.

So I tell her, "If you want to go to this school, you make the first call, and I'll take it from there." And she does. And I do.

It is a golden day in June, when I drive four hours from Sayville, Long Island to Hancock, New York. A tiny village upstate of just under 1000 residents, it is in the middle of nowhere. Crossing the Delaware River near town, I follow a hilly blacktop road for a few miles, then turn onto a tiny dirt road that meanders down to the school.

After a meeting with the principal, I am given the tour where I see that the place is a farm with dorms for about 100 kids. Classrooms, athletic fields, and a small lake make up the rest of the campus. And that's it.

In the miniscule town center, I had noticed a few businesses—an Indian trading post and a cafe. There are a couple of motels along the main road, lots of woods, and a few other houses nearby. I'm guessing the kids can't get into too much trouble here.

I am invited to sit with one of the "families" at a community lunch table and observe the school in action. The students are divided into six groups or "families" that sit together at meals, live together, and help each other.

While they are eating their burgers and fries, the staff discusses specific issues that have come up. One student is dealing with being dishonest and now everyone is listening. At first I find it a harsh approach, but as the conversation continues, I observe the incorporation of the 12 Steps. Also, I realize that the staff members are also in recovery so they share their experiences with the students. Much of the conversation and support comes from their peers.

Mid-meal a phone call comes in—one of the students has tried to run away. A few volunteers are selected to go with staff members in the truck to find the escapee. Even the gun carrying locals don't scare the kids who are determined to run away. Later, I will find out that parents have to sign a consent form to give permission for the school to actively search for their runaway child.

I understand the place to be tough and caring at the same time, so I sign Suzanne up, accepting funds from my mother that she has been saving for a rainy day. I tell her it's pouring.

Since Suzanne will start in September, she stays with a friend in CT for the summer. The principal has told me that in order to ensure that she shows up, we have to make certain that all her other options run out. That had already started to happen. No one else could offer her a place to live.

Throughout the summer, Suzanne and I are in touch by phone and by mail. We are polite and civil, but I am cautious. I have been so angry and frustrated, but I allow myself to be optimistic about this school after seeing with my own eyes how things work. I'm not sure exactly how Suzanne feels, but she is willing to give this place a chance. After all, it was her idea. I figure that's a plus.

✳ ✳ ✳

On a cloudless sunny day at the end of August, Suzanne takes Metro North from Connecticut to Grand Central Station where we rendezvous and begin our three-hour drive from NYC to the Family School. It's the third stop on the "rehab" tour, though technically not a rehab, but a school with extra support. We ride mostly in silence as we leave the city. Farms with grazing horses and cows dot the green landscape and hills emerge. I have told her that she only has to stay a year, which is a lie because it's a minimum 18 months. But I don't want her to change her mind.

Lots of parents bring their children kicking and screaming. Some are in need of escort services. I expect that our peaceful journey, with the little lie stuck in, may be one of the more pleasant arrivals. We are not what anyone would describe as close at this time, but we are polite. Neighborly. Our parting is matter of fact. This is what she has agreed to and so this is what is done. I sign the document giving permission for the school to go after her if she runs away. She never does.

During the drive home, I feel myself relax a bit. My shoulders come down from my ears. I am able to notice the beauty of the rural wilderness and feel grateful that I get to experience it.

After a week, I get the first five-minute phone call. Because the calls are short, the students get right to the issues at hand. "I'm working on being honest," Suzanne offers. "And can you please send some socks?" Fall comes earlier upstate and it is already getting chilly. There is no time for small talk. The phone calls with parents become the reward.

Over time, we begin to connect and soften with these calls. The truth is that we miss each other and want things to be better. For the first time I start to feel some deep relief that Suzanne is in a safe place, going to school, and getting help that has the potential to stick. It's the most "normal" either of us has felt in years and now I have more time for Lisa. Suzanne will turn 17 in a couple of months. I am hoping she can graduate from this school.

After the first month, I am invited to a meeting with Suzanne and her counselor, Ann. They do something called the "honesty list" where Suzanne has to tell me everything that I didn't know about the bad things she did. My brain had blocked out most of the details, not wanting to remember all the drugs she used and the items she stole to buy them. How lucky was she that she never got in trouble with the law!

This is a lot to handle, but I trust the counselor. Ann talks about forgiveness, how she had been abused by her father. Everyone in her family had been, but she was the only one able to forgive him in the end. And it was crucial to her lasting sobriety, she says.

When I leave after lunch, my brain is buzzing with revelations from the "honesty list." Dumped on me all at once, the reality of Suzanne's exploits starts to sink in. I feel shaky. I don't know what to do with these uncomfortable thoughts swirling around my head, and I have a four-hour drive ahead of me. Guilt sinks in. I should have been able to do more for my daughter. I should have known what was going on. I'm her mother dammit! I get the list thrown at me and then I have to go figure it out on my own? That doesn't feel right.

On the way to the highway, there's a fairly sharp turn on a high embankment in these Catskill Mountain foothills. Looking down, I think about how easy it would be if I just let my car drive over it. That would stop the guilt and the anger.

But I don't.

Instead, the next day I call the counselor and tell her how bad I felt after that session, and how there should be some kind of processing for parents who have to get behind the wheel of a car after an honesty list. I may have yelled at her, just a teensy bit, maybe more. She apologizes.

From this point on, I come prepared with distraction for the ride home. For every trip, I purchase a brand new CD, which I don't unwrap until then. This way I have something to look forward to and I can focus on getting home in one piece. This allows me to process the day more peacefully.

CHAPTER 8

Lost and Found

Back home, I stare at Suzanne's rented oboe, sitting unused in its plastic case next to her bed. The Family School has a choir, but no instrumental program. Sadly, I realize that it's time to return the oboe, but I resist. This is not part of the plan I had for my daughter. The oboe was supposed to be Suzanne's ticket to college.

Not everybody plays oboe. She will be special and desired and many scholarships will be offered to get her into the best schools. She will learn from my mistake (giving up the clarinet in 9th grade) and continue playing, even when it doesn't feel "cool." I'll make sure of that.

It was a solid plan, but the Universe had other ideas. Singing at the Family School will have to be enough for now.

Suzanne's musical talents had become part of her soul. At age five, she began to learn piano. In elementary school when she took up the oboe, she played in the special jazz band and I never got tired of hearing their rendition of "Stand by Me," which they worked on all year, every year. Mr. Kaunitz, the beloved director of the regular band, would gloriously wave his baton over the squeaks and out of tune notes, as if he were conducting professionals in the philharmonic. The kids felt like pros.

In junior high and high school, she took private vocal and oboe lessons and was selected for the elite Show Choir. As a member of the marching band's flag team in high school, she ran up and down the football field, joyously waving her flag, feeling free. In the midst of all the chaos at home, music helped build her self-esteem.

Even with all these supportive and positive experiences, life wasn't easy. Not at all. One time the vocal teacher had her sing "Sometimes I Feel like a Motherless Child" for a recital. I'm pretty sure Mrs. M. was sending a direct message to me, but I wasn't ready to hear it. I was in my anarchistic, rebellious period and was spending too much time away from home with my new boyfriend.

So it is a somber ride to the music store in Patchogue where I will turn in the oboe for good. The sadness that comes over me is more than a sadness about the oboe. It is an acknowledgement of grief. Not much of anything has turned out the way I expected it to.

I park the car in front of the shop and dash in. It takes less than five minutes to let the oboe go. I get back in the car and cry the whole way home.

***

The Family School turns out to be transformational for Suzanne and for our relationship. She benefits from the structure and she thrives in her academics.

The infrequent visits and calls are precious. When we are apart we grow, explore, and expand individually. When we are together we connect more deeply. And it is sweet.

We exchange letters and cards the old-fashioned way. The ones from me are filled with positive and encouraging messages. I am just starting to dabble in artwork and I love to send her my rudimentary drawings. I attend my first sweat lodge. She goes to a choral competition. Years later Suzanne will present me with a scrapbook to honor our loving relationship. It is filled with photos and the letters and cards I had sent her that summer when she was in Connecticut and at the Family School.

I pick her up for a weekend visit and we stay at a log cabin-style motel near town. I take a photo of her sleeping, snuggled under the bright pink and green floral blanket. *Why do parents love to watch their kids sleep?* We meander through back roads allowing ourselves to get a little lost. Sitting by the Delaware River, we watch the trout fishermen, soaking up their calm. We have cheeseburgers in a local Mom and Pop dinette and share stories from the past. There is laughter. I can feel both our hearts soften.

In June, nine months later, Lisa and I go to pick Suzanne up for a weekend adventure. We have tickets to the

Clearwater Music Festival on the Hudson River. We see Dar Williams our favorite singer/songwriter. The joy of this reunion is palpable. I have photos of this time with smiles like I hadn't seen in years. Two sisters reunited in pure love. Laying on a blanket, heads on each other's bellies, laughing and cuddling, we feel like a functional family. "Let's meet every year at the Clearwater," Lisa says. "No matter what is going on." And we nod our heads in agreement, although it never happens. Because the Universe has other plans.

The next day at the festival, an afternoon thunderstorm appears out of nowhere. Instead of running for cover, the girls splash in the puddles while giggling like little kids. Their tee shirts and shorts get drenched and their hair plasters down their backs. I watch pure freedom. They are being children. They are being sisters. It's a moment I never thought possible, but dreamed of.

For another visit, Lisa and I pick up Suzanne and we make a trip to Temple University in Philadelphia to check out the music therapy program at the Esther Boyer College of Music. I have researched this kind of program and it seems to be a good fit for Suzanne and somewhat affordable, since it's a state school. We go to the bookstore and Suzanne buys a Temple jacket. A clarity comes over me and I'm sure she will be accepted.

When I drive her to the interview/ audition a few months later, I advise her to be honest, to just tell her story of the last few years and how music has helped her get through everything.

And as I predict, she gets in. She graduates from the Family School in December, but stays in the area an extra semester to pick up some college credits at Broome County Community College before the transfer to Philadelphia where she will begin her double life.

College student by day. AA member by night.

CHAPTER 9

Found and Lost

Suzanne flourishes in college. By day, it's classes, where she shines in her academics. Her new dorm friends, also music majors, provide a rich social experience. A wonderful boyfriend, who wants to become a filmmaker, comes into her life. By night at AA meetings, she has a whole new set of like-minded friends in recovery.

I visit her and stay in the dorm with her when her roommate is away. While she is sleeping, I wake up earlier than most of the college students and sketch her sleeping. It is peaceful on a Saturday morning in the dorm. And I can't get enough of sleeping Suzanne.

She brings me to her meetings to show me off. We go out to hear music and have meals. We are enjoying our time together. She is sober and thriving. And so is our relationship.

There are other visits when I drive in from Long Island just to hear her perform and go home that same night fighting highway hypnosis on the New Jersey Turnpike. But it is worth it.

Back home, though, Lisa is sinking—like the Titanic. (She's obsessed with the movie and has seen it six times.) She has lost interest in school and doesn't want to go. One morning I sit on the edge of her bed and watch her trying to bury herself under the covers. "Family School?" I ask. She nods. She sees what it has done for Suzanne and she wants that too.

We make it happen. This time her father volunteers to chip in, as he also sees what it has done for Suzanne. In addition to her academics, Lisa gets to be a cheerleader, continue ballet, and sing in the choir. When Suzanne and I go up to visit her, we savor the time that we are together as a family.

When I am alone with Lisa we drive to the mall in Binghamton. Lisa loves a mall. She'll walk for miles in a mall. In the car ride back to the motel, as the stars begin to glow in the deepest darkness of rural New York, we listen to Enya and sing some new songs that she has learned in choir. Some of them are rounds and we sing together while holding hands.

The Family School gives me back my children. It also gives me back myself.

While the girls are safe and doing well, major changes happen for me. First, I "reclaim" the house. I tear up carpets and rip off every piece of wallpaper that my ex-husband hung. He was obsessed with it. Wallpaper, wallpaper everywhere. I repaint the walls and enjoy the feeling of my arm moving the paint onto the surface. It is the first time in my life that I paint anything. And I am inspired to explore this more.

After I begin art classes in Manhattan, the dining room becomes my art studio. I do batiking on the floor and practice painting on canvas paper which I hang on the walls.

I buy a few new Ikea pieces to freshen up the house, then invite some friends over. We have a "house reclaiming ceremony" where we burn candles and bang pots and sage the place from top to bottom, chasing out all the negative energy that may be lingering in corners. These strong, compassionate women help me dismantle the marriage bed and get that to the curb for trash pick up. They also carry the ex's "drinking chair" up the basement stairs to join the bed pieces at the curb. The house is now mine.

It is eight years after the divorce and with both kids doing well, there is more space in my brain for new ideas. I decide that although I love teaching, the world is opening up. When I allow my brain to shift into new possibilites, lomi lomi, Hawaiian massage, finds its way into my life. Within months, I decide to leave teaching, sell the newly reclaimed house, and move to Manhattan to do that work.

Seven months later in June of 2000, Lisa graduates from the Family School after spending two years there and comes to live with me in my tiny little apartment on East 85th

Street, where we have a precious reunion. She gets a part-time job at Ann Taylor on Third Avenue and begins her first semester in Hunter College just a few subway stops away. We cook together and snuggle a lot. She begins to purchase Christmas gifts with her Anne Taylor discount. She gets her first credit card. And her first tattoo, a tribal design around her belly button. She wonders what will happen to it when she becomes pregnant one day.

But she never finds out. She doesn't make it to Christmas. After we are together for three months, she dies.

At 3AM on October 8, 2000, there is a car accident in Hamilton, New Jersey where three recent graduates of the Family School are instantly killed. One of them is Lisa. Her friend Amy, the driver, gets distracted and the car hits a tree, resulting in an uncontrollable fire. In the middle of the night, after attending a sober comedy club and returning to Amy's house, they had decided they were hungry and piled back into the car in search of food. The plan was to drive upstate that morning for a little reunion at the Family School, but that never happened..

Her last words to me in a phone call—" I love you Mommy."

The morning of the accident, I go to the park by the river to have my coffee and read a magazine. When I return to my apartment, there are two police officers waiting to give me the news. Hours later, after I have called Suzanne and we have gone to Queens to tell my mother, I make a decision. The horrific accident will not define Lisa. She will forever be my sweet, funny, loving daughter. In that moment I am clear that any time I spend thinking of the ugly details will rob me of the best of Lisa. It is a knowing that just comes over me. I don't talk about fault or blame or anything that cannot change what happened.

Lisa's father arranges to have the funeral on Long Island and Suz stays with me for a week. The Principal of the Family School asks me what I need. "The Choir," I answer without any hesitation. And they make it happen. It is "Open Mic" for Lisa and there are other participants. I am completely out of my mind but manage to stand in front of everyone to invite them to share. My newly sober ex-husband stands behind me with his arms on my shoulders. He doesn't say anything and I can't remember what I say, but he is there and I feel his support.

We are all very much in shock and haven't felt anything deeply yet. When Suzanne goes back to Philly, she leaves me a note. *"How will we do on our own without each other?"* I go back to teaching math at the Young Women's Leadership School of East Harlem, where I had taken a *respectable j*ob when Lisa moved in.

Suzanne returns to Temple University. I think being busy will be good for us. What do I know? I have never lost a child.

At first there is disbelief—like it didn't happen, and Lisa would walk through the door any minute. It becomes real about six weeks later at a Compassionate Friends meeting where I have to speak the details of her passing to a room full of people. Unbearably real. Later that night a couple of friends meet me at my apartment, where I have the biggest and deepest full body heaving cry I have ever had in my life. The kind of cry where you think that you have left the world and may never come back. If you don't know what I'm talking about, that's a good thing.

And even with the depth of the pain, there is a part of my brain that lets me do mundane things like get out of bed, take a shower, eat, and teach math to middle school kids.... for a while.

After the first big cry, I cry often. Everywhere. I manage to hold it together until I am walking home or until I am on the bus or subway, where I cry indiscriminately, because I am unambiguously sad. There are a few weeks where I am angry—not at any person, just angry that it happened, but mostly it is the tears that flow.

In the early weeks, there is a telephone conversation with Suzanne about grieving. At this point I am anything but an expert. I just tell her what I am experiencing, but to be honest, I am so overwhelmed by sadness that I cannot be very helpful to Suzanne. I tell her that I save my crying for when I leave work, hoping that she can do the same.

Everyone grieves differently. Years later I will learn that *she felt like she had lost a limb.*

Six months later, in spring, I hit the wall. I can't get out of bed. My grief has finally caught up with me. It's time for standardized testing and I have been assigned "test coordinator," an additional duty. My brain can't handle it. Neither can my body. I am on overload. Something has to change. I want to teach part time, but NYC doesn't allow that, so in April, I resign.

Meanwhile, in Philadelphia, Suzanne relapses. She takes her first drink with dinner on New Year's Eve, end of 2000, but she keeps it from me. She is 21 years old and a sophomore in college.

Suzanne visits in early spring and gets to meet my new boyfriend, who is loving and sweet, and generous. We all hang out at a bar at the corner of York and 85th Street, singing Billy Joel songs and having a beer or two. That's when I see that she's drinking again. Because we are both out of our minds with grief and finding ways to cope, I don't have the energy to call her out. It doesn't seem that bad, certainly not ominous. I think about it and decide that I like having one daughter alive, in whatever condition she is in. Having a sweet time in a bar feels okay. And I am happy to have even some minutes of okay. *Maybe she can drink normally.* I wonder.

When 9/11 happens, almost a year after Lisa's passing, everything escalates.

CHAPTER 10

After 9/11/2001

The ex and I learn from Suzanne's friends that her drinking is out of control, but she won't ask for help. We travel together from New York to Philly hoping that this grand gesture of concern will be enough to cause her to open up to us. And maybe ask for help as she has done in the past.

Before we see her, we walk along South Street like we are still married. We visit the new age, spiritual shop, Garland Of Letters, one of my favorites, where we buy her a stone with the word TRUTH on it, hoping that it will inspire her to share. She has to. We are optimistic.

"What are you two doing here?" she says flatly when we show up at her doorstep. She is surprised, but it's not a strong reaction. The muscles on one side of her face attempt a half smile. She won't talk. She won't give us answers about anything. I flash back to the way she was when we brought her to the therapist after her suicide attempt at age 12. Resistant. Toughest nut to crack. We knew this wasn't good. The trip back to New York is pretty quiet.

Christmas, 2001

The phone rings about 9 AM. It is my ex-husband. "Merry Christmas, Suzanne's on heroin." Best Christmas ever.

What happens afterward is pretty foggy. There's a detox, a rehab on Long Island, and a halfway house in the East Village. While she is at the halfway house, she reconnects with an old boyfriend from the Family School, who has also relapsed and she ends up back on heroin. When she is kicked out of the halfway house, I ask my mother to help out, because I am completely overwhelmed by grief of losing one child and exhausted from trying to help the other.

Grandma Lila comes through. She lets Suzanne stay with her In Queens and chaperones her to the required drug tests and AA meetings in Manhattan. Mom waits in the dingy LIRR waiting room with the ripped seats and the derelicts, hoping and praying that Suzanne will return. She always does. Hopefully, she will stay clean so she can qualify to get back into the halfway house.

Unfortunately, the pull of the drug and the boyfriend are strong. They end up in a dumpy apartment in a run down section of Williamsburg. It takes a few months but eventually they become sick of living life addicted to drugs and decide in the summer of 2002 to go down to his mother's place in Nashville and try to get into a methadone program.

Before Suzanne leaves for Nashville, I give her two things—my car and a credit card. For numerous logical reasons, it is not advisable to give a person with addictions either one of those items, but there is something in my gut that tells me to do it. I don't need the car—Suzanne does. She needs to get down to Nashville to get sober. The credit card, I tell her, is for emergencies.

It is around this time that I find the Al-Anon parents meeting in Manhattan, right in my neighborhood. I flip between support groups—Compassionate Friends, for parents who have lost children and the other, for parents who are dealing with their child's addictions. At the latter one, loss of a child is the biggest fear. In a church basement, an experienced member with fully grown children shared that all four of her kids were addicted and all four got sober, but not because of anything she did. This was hopeful.

In addition to attending the meetings, I continue practicing Hawaiian massage. Even though I might be a sobbing mess beforehand, by the end of the session, I feel better. Many other people who do healing work are curious about lomi lomi so there are frequent exchanges. I get to receive other kinds of massage, reiki, EMDR, and grief therapy. A face painter friend encourages me to do more artwork, so I take more art classes to express my grief. I throw paint onto canvas, paint with my feet, and create giant collages that look like altars.

Although initial reports from Nashville are positive, everything falls apart there too. When Suzanne calls me, she goes on and on about all her problems. It's chaotic. She's living in a house with strangers, who are not nice people. It is hard to hear, but I listen. Because I am attending my meetings, I am able to say to her these words: "You know what you need to do and when you are ready, you will do it." When I hang up the phone I fall apart, but while talking to my daughter, I am strong.

On an easel in my apartment, I keep what I call a "visual prayer," a photo of Suzanne surrounded by colorful and beautiful designs. Every day I add something new. Some gold stars, a bit of pink nail polish, some glitter. I visualize her healthy and being taken care of by angels, God, and the Universe. There is also a spoken prayer, that I say out loud directly to Lisa— *Watch out for you sister!* It is not so much a prayer as it is a command, like a mother might say to one sibling about the other one as they are going out to play. I can't prove that Lisa has any influence on the Other Side, but I know it in my heart.

One day in Nashville, after many nights of taking drugs, Suzanne falls down a flight of stairs and has what she refers to as a "mystical experience." An angel or God or the Universe or Lisa tells her it's time. It's time to "do the thing she knows she has to do." She starts the drive home.

The car I gave her gets her home. She uses the credit card for gas. It is the only time she uses it.

* * *

It takes a minute for her to find her way back to sobriety. She goes out of her way to Queens to "borrow" hundreds of dollars from my mother's dresser. She then proceeds to Philadelphia, where she ends up at the film festival where her ex-boyfriend's film, the one he made about her, debuts. She is embarrassed and ashamed to see herself in decline. After she nods off in front of his parents, she ends up running out and driving around the city aimlessly until she calls her best friend, Lauren, who takes her to a safe place. Here she declares that she wants to get sober. And it is Lauren who makes the call to Suzanne's dad, then drives four hours from Philly to Rocky Point, Long Island where he lives. This is where she gets sober This is the one that sticks ...for 11 years.

CHAPTER 11

The Golden Years

Fall, 2008. Philadelphia

"What about Philly?" Suzanne looks at me with her big green puppy eyes from the other side of the cafe table. After nine years in Manhattan, I am thinking of moving to Brooklyn or Queens. The current financial crisis has slowed my work, but not lowered my rent.

I've taken the Greyhound Bus to Philly, just for the day. We're in the latest hip area, Northern Liberties. Suzanne is now sober for five years and thriving. After finishing up her music therapy program at Temple she earned a BS in nursing in a fast-tracked program at Jefferson University where she now works. She loves nursing. All is well. So well that my daughter wants me to move near her.

What about Philly? I wonder. I had never considered it before. I notice some local newspapers on a shelf along the wall and pick one up, flipping to the back pages where rentals are listed and read aloud: "Apartment Sale, Rittenhouse Square, $900." Suzanne grabs the local weekly out of my hands. "We're calling RIGHT NOW!!" She knows that this is a very good price for a lovely neighborhood and right smack in the middle of Center City. And I know that it's a bit more than half of what I'm paying now in Manhattan.

She makes the call and the rental agent happens to be free at that moment, so we drop everything and dash over there to take a look. It feels like Fate.

The historic high-rise building on the corner of Spruce and 19th is just a block south of the famous Rittenhouse Square, a lovely park in the city. There is a door attendant and 18 floors. The apartment on the 6th floor is a studio, and it's four times the size of my NYC place, with an eat-in kitchen and a wall of closets off the main room. The main room has space for my bed and a couch. And its windows face west, so I can watch the sun set, even from the bathroom.

Standing in the kitchen, I feel grateful. Grateful that we have been through so much and come out on the other side. Grateful that my daughter wants me to be close to her and I want her to be close to me. There is a whoosh of energy that comes over me—maybe it is God or the Universe or Lisa, but I decide right then to take the place.

Two months later I am a Philadelphian.

We live within walking distance and see each other frequently. Sometimes we randomly bump into each other on the street, where I am thrilled to get an unexpected hug.

I might find Suzanne at a table outside a restaurant. She is always surrounded by a group of friends from college, work, running, or her meetings. She enjoys showing me off to her friends who tell me that they have heard much about me. Other times, I spot her jogging down the street, her ponytail swaying from side to side as she runs. We both love these random encounters.

After 3 1/2 years in the high-rise, tenants get a visit from the "Assessor," after which rents are increased by a third and many residents, including me, are forced out. It doesn't take long to find a beautiful second floor walk-up close by in an old grey stone house from the 1880's on quiet tree-lined St. James Place. It faces the backyard with a southern exposure just like my NYC place and has a giant flowering magnolia that blooms in spring. The large bay window allows sun to fill the room with light. And it's even closer to Suzanne's apartment. I take it immediately.

As we live easily in the same city, we go about our lives. I am still back and forth to NYC for weekend face painting and dance programs. Suzanne shines, sponsoring newer AA members and helping where she can. Her running interest increases and she even does marathons. But her love life has had some challenges. After a few unsuccessful relationships, Suzanne, at my suggestion, experiments with being "single and celibate." This ends when she meets her future husband, a surgical resident at the hospital.

The boyfriend frequently stays at her place with his dog, Dutchy, a sweet senior pitbull. It's just a seven minute walk from my new place to her apartment, so I become the dog walker when they cannot get home in time. Dutchy and I bond and my granddog is patient with me as I figure out how to work her collar and leash.

When Dutchy dies, during cancer surgery, Suzanne is inconsolable. So, they get Mulligan, a younger more rambunctious male pitbull, and I have a new granddog. Mully and I play fetch with a tennis ball. He doesn't like to give up the ball, so we also play tug. We go for walks and I teach him some manners. Even as he salivates, he learns to sit while waiting for me to feed him. And I send Suzanne videos of her dog while she pursues her masters in Nurse Anesthesia at Drexel University.

I call these years in Philly the *golden years*. We have come out of the earlier chaos. Chaos feels like another lifetime, long ago.

CHAPTER 12

Nothing Gold Can Stay

8/29/14

The date is embossed in gold on a souvenir matchbox from a family wedding. It isn't everyone who gets a memento from the day her child relapses.

Also embossed on the matchbox, in block letters, are the words, *BEST DAY EVER. EVER* is at least double the size of the other words. I'm not kidding.

That matchbox will stay for nine years in my gold Kate Spade evening bag, an outstanding purchase from a consignment shop (it was a glorious find, that bag) until I rediscover it.

The wedding is held at a country club on the north shore of Long Island with pristine landscaped grounds and gardens lush with the fullness of the season. Floral bouquets of fuchsia and yellow decorate the room and tables overflow with scrumptious delicacies.

But Suzanne and the fiancé have been fighting and he has asked for the ring back. At the wedding the drama continues. Most of the guests are oblivious, but my mother and I are concerned. Even though she has had 11 years of sobriety, relapse is always possible. We worry if a major emotional event like this one could set a relapse in motion.

After the dessert table rolls out, Suzanne comes up to me. She seems hesitant to speak. "I had a cigarette," she offers, her head down. Smoking is usually a sign that she is dealing with some overwhelming emotions. "Don't worry," I tell her. "Everything will be okay. You will feel better tomorrow." I'm trying to be as positive as I can. She thanks me for understanding.

Later Suzanne tells me that she also has taken some "sips of champagne." I don't want to think it's a big deal, hoping that it is just situational, a minor slip, and that she will get herself back on track the next day, but I am scared.

Just a few weeks later, the engagement is back on and Suzanne and I are walking down busy Market Street to Old City to meet her fiancé for some spicy Chinese food at Han Dynasty. Suddenly, Suzanne stops in the middle of the sidewalk. Above the noise of sirens blaring and horns beeping, she turns, and looks at me straight on. "Mom, I think it's okay for me to drink."

This declaration is unexpected. My gut stiffens and my mouth gets dry. Every nerve has been activated. I feel the adrenalin and cortisol course through my body. In an instant my brain flashes back to all the prior chaos and trauma that came with her addiction as a teenager and the relapse after Lisa died. It brings back the powerlessness I felt in my dysfunctional marriage. The next day I have my first AFib episode.

I manage to get through the evening watching my daughter drink two glasses of champagne. I am thinking that already she has progressed from sips to full glasses. I feel the need to say something, but what to say, and how to say it? "I don't think that this is a good idea." The words stick in my throat. I look to her fiancé for support. "Don't worry Mom, we got this," she says. They both seem to feel that they have it under control. Suzanne gives me and her fiancé permission to tell her when we think the drinking gets out of hand. My spicy Chinese food is tasteless that night.

The next day, I don't know what to do or how to handle my fears. I decide to dance it out at Koresh School of Dance. Dancing is good therapy for me, usually. It's a hot day in September, and I consume a giant heavily caffeinated iced coffee before class. In an unairconditoned studio, the modern jazz class is vigorous.

Strangely, I feel a little light-headed on the way home. I stop in a deli at 21st and Locust to get a large bottle of water. Maybe I am de-hydrated. It is just a couple of blocks from the dance studio to my house, but I have to stop every half block to catch my breath. This worries me.

When I get home, I lie on my bed, but every time I start to get up, my heart beats fast and I feel faint, so I lie back down. I can actually feel the thumping of my heart. I think

I may be having a heart attack, but I'm not sure. I call Suzanne who's at a wedding with her fiancé. They will know what I should do. Suzanne stays on the phone with me, while her fiancé calls an ambulance, so I know they think it's serious.

I realize that the front door to my building will be locked and the only way in is for someone on the inside to open it, so I manage to go down the two flights and leave the door ajar and go back up. *This is a pretty good heart attack,* I think, *if I am having one.* I had forgotten that there was a fire escape entrance on my hallway, but the EMT's know about it. So when I get back upstairs, they are waiting for me.

My heart rate is 200, which is no bueno, even I know that. The EMT tells me that he is going to inject my heart with a medication that will stop it for a minute and then start it again. A heart re-boot. Hopefully I don't die in between. I feel intense sensation, pressure, like there's a waterfall on my chest after the administration of the drug. Then they help me down the stairs and put me in the ambulance.

Suzanne and her fiancé leave the wedding and meet me at Jefferson Hospital, where they work. They are at their best here and they don't take their eyes off the monitors. I am given the royal treatment and stay overnight for observation. I tell all the doctors about the giant coffee, the vigorous dance class, and the overly hot room—but I leave out the part where my daughter is drinking again, after eleven years of sobriety, and how that has affected me emotionally. They say words like "perfect storm" and think that maybe that's that. I hope they are right.

CHAPTER 13

Ups and Downs

"Don't sacrifice your soul for a wedding," I say to Suzanne and her future husband over shrimp pils pils at Dimitri's, a local Greek seafood restaurant. "It's just not worth it."

Even though the couple has reconciled, their wedding plans create conflict. I can sense that they are not on the same page. The only detail they are certain of is that I will officiate. That's where the agreement ends.

The groom wants a big fancy event, but there's no money to support this. They have huge school loans and my daughter will be carrying most of the financial weight. Also, there is a lack of clarity about the contribution that his parents will make. He assumes that they will be contributing quite a bit. I have made it clear that I will buy the wedding dress, but do not have the funds to contribute any more. My mom offers to chip in some cash.

As it turns out, the future in-laws are tapped out after paying for their daughter's lavish affair just a few months before and contribute nothing. This escalates the tension that seems to go beyond finances.

At some point, it is decided to downsize the wedding, but only after my mother had placed a $6000 non-refundable deposit on a catering hall out on Long Island, that the future in-laws had encouraged the couple to book *before* they gave them the news about not contributing.

Because of the downsizing, it will be immediate family and a few friends at the ceremony and celebration, now booked in a restaurant on Long Island. The groom's extended family can't hide their disappointment and this causes some hard feelings all around. Suzanne tells me how disillusioned she has become with the groom's family.

In November my mom and I have a party for Suzanne and her girlfriends at a Mexican restaurant in Philly—not exactly a bachelorette party, but just a pre-wedding celebration. There's a lot of alcohol consumed and the next day I hear that a few friends had taken Suzanne out for an after party, where she overindulges.

A few close friends, who had witnessed her first relapse, have an intervention for her at her apartment the next day to express their concern. Now, I'm not alone because more people are worried about Suzanne's future and her marriage. I'm feeling relieved that I have some support.

Every morning I do a guided meditation asking for help from my angels. It feels as if everything is out of my hands and spinning uncontrollably. I attempt to be as supportive as possible, without telling my daughter what to do, as I'd very much like to.

As the date of the wedding gets closer, Suzanne is visibly upset. She sobs but she has no words to explain the tears. I surmise that she is upset about the absence of her sister or her estranged father. That would make sense. But I am in the dark. *I wish I could help you, Suzanne,* but I'm not seeing a way in.

"If there is anything that doesn't feel right," I tell her, "you can change your mind at any time. And the world will not end."

She doesn't change her mind.

Suzanne wakes up to an unseasonably warm rainy and dismal December wedding day. She is unhappy with her droopy hair caused by the humidity. It has been a few months since the relapse and I still haven't told my mother. She's hiding her drinking from me, but I notice the open bottle of champagne in her dressing room. I am not fooled.

Amazingly, the event goes well. The in-laws walk Suzanne down the aisle and Lauren, her best friend, is the maid of honor. I had helped them with their vows prior to the ceremony, but they had kept them secret from each other. The ceremony is lovely, heartfelt, and intimate. I'm feeling hopeful.

I've created a playlist and we dance a bit. Even my mom, who is 86, gets on the dance floor. Suzanne, a bit tipsy from the champagne, dips Mom just a little too far and she falls. Mom gets a bump on her leg that doesn't go away for months.

Suzanne feels terrible.

I still don't tell my mother that Suzanne is drinking.

* * *

Six months later on a brilliant May day, we are on our way to a mother/daughter weekend at Kripalu Yoga Center In the Berkshire Mountains. Somewhere on Old Stockbridge Road, just a few miles from our destination, Suzanne tells me about a trip she is planning in early 2016 to Tanzania to hike Mt. Kilimanjaro.

This will happen after she moves to Dallas for her husband's new position. None of her friends have expressed any interest in going, so she invites me.

I say yes without hesitation. When your daughter asks you to go to Africa, you say Yes and figure it out later.

We talk continuously during the weekend as we walk through the woods and take yoga classes. Some of the hard issues come up between us and I admit that I could be a better listener. But we don't talk about her drinking, the elephant in the room. Even though she is still drinking, it seems like it's calmed down a bit. I want to believe that she has it under control, but I know better. I've been through early relapse before.

At the bookstore Suzanne purchases some books on healing foods. She brings them back to our room and opens up a giant tome that must weigh at least ten pounds. She is planning ahead. "I might get a doctorate in nutrition from Harvard," she says as she begins to read. "Anything is possible," I tell her. She is already a CRNA (Certified Registered Nurse Anesthetist). I tell her how proud I am of all her accomplishments. And that I am looking forward to her continuing to evolve and follow her dreams

CHAPTER 14

Texas Two-Step

Dallas, November, 2015

I am visiting Suzanne and her husband for the first time. The kids are taking me to an authentic Texas Two-Step event because they know how much I love to dance. I packed a new pair of boots purchased specifically for this event. I'm ready! There isn't a dance I've met that I don'l like.

Suz and I are picking up a few items for dinner when she spots the mango sale and buys half a dozen. Who can resist a sale? Her husband will use them later for his special mojitos. Back at the apartment, Suzanne begins chopping and slicing vegetables for our dinner and the husband brings out the blender for his special drink. I am given a couple of tasks, but mostly I feel they want me out of the way, so I play with my granddog Mully. When I drop ice cubes from the fridge onto the floor, he chomps on them, then looks up at me for more. This is a fun game.

With a significant pour of the rum, the husband makes sure the women present get pretty tipsy. I had already accepted Suzanne in relapse mode, which included watching her have a drink. I'm a lightweight when it comes to any alcohol. Suzanne is noticeably affected and we are all giddy until a ceramic bowl slips from Suzanne's fingers and lands on her big toe. It hurts but she doesn't want to go to the emergency room. Instead, the surgeon husband happens to have some pain medication which he injects into her foot, more than once. They insist on calling an Uber to take us to the dance and make this evening happen.

This particular event is in a venue the size of a roller rink, where everyone shows great respect for the dance and dresses the part. Authentic Western boots, hats and lots of fringed skirts and shirts. My mock western boots will have to do.

I think that dancing will be the main focus of the night, but for the next couple hours, I watch, in disbelief, while Suzanne's husband feeds her numerous rum and cokes for "anesthetic" purposes.

Texans take their Two-Step seriously and the teacher reprimands a laughing sloppy drunk woman while a full room of people stare in silence and disbelief. It's Suzanne causing the ruckus and she can hardly control herself. My heart aches witnessing this.

I try as much detachment as I can muster and have a couple of dances with a well-skilled Two-Stepper. As I am solidly led around the floor, I begin to pick up the dance, in spite of the family chaos. People are moving around the dance floor non-stop. It is the Texas I was hoping to see, but not the Suzanne. I hadn't seen this Suzanne in years. My muscles tense and my mind flashes back to the chaotic days of deep addiction. Maybe this is a one off, because of her toe pain. But I'm scared. *What's happening when I'm not here?* I wonder.

I leave Dallas the next day and let things settle down. A few days later, I make a call to Suzanne and express my concern about the excessive drinking. As a parent of an adult, it is a delicate balance that one must find, but at least she knows how I feel. I definitely can't control her actions.

Eventually the toe nail turns black and falls off, the marriage ends, and the drinking continues.

CHAPTER 15

African Adventure

After the Texas-Two step fiasco, Suzanne begins to train for the Kilimanjaro trek coming up in a few months. There is no discussion of her quitting drinking or going back to AA meetings. It seems as if she is determined to be healthy enough for the trek, which is encouraging. Training includes long runs, trail hikes, and yoga classes. She reads up on high-altitude climbing and gets the suggested medications. She travels to Colorado a few times for practice hikes at Pike's Peak (14,000 feet).

There's a lot of communication between us as we plan our African adventure. I am going mainly as support for her climb and I will remain at the hotel. There's a possibility of volunteering at the local orphanage, a charity connected to the tour company that plans everything for us, including a four-day safari after the climb. We are both extremely excited for the trip.

Traveling together from Philly on Qatar airlines, we are treated to a luxurious experience. In the cabin's romantic pink and purple glow, we have a whole row to ourselves, perfect for naps during the 20-hour flight. Because Suzanne hadn't seen one of my favorite movies, *Out of Africa,* we watch it. It seems like there's a meal or snack every two hours. While I doze, Suzanne watches *Everest.* She is already thinking of her next adventure—hiking Everest's base camp.

Because I like to plan some breathing room into my trips, we arrange for a free day at the hotel the day before the trek. The gated hotel grounds sit just outside of Moshi, the main town. Lush plants, bubbling fountains, a sparkling pool, and an outdoor covered eating area welcome us. The main building and the guest accomodations are arranged around the periphery. In our room, a pair of canopy beds with bright crimson bedspreads invites us to rest. Mosquito nets cover the beds and billow gently from the ceiling fan's breeze. I exhale. The showers aren't perfect with little pressure and limited hot water, but we don't mind after the lengthy trip. We spend the day relaxing around the pool, doing laps and chatting as we recover from the flight.

"Mama, let me show you the mountain." Juma, one of our waiters, takes me by the hand when he senses my apprehension about Suzanne's climb. I had shown off with a little bit of my practiced Swahili, which got some smiles and chuckles from the waiters. I like them. Juma walks me out of the gated complex to the dirt road where giant Mt. Kilimanjaro looms like a god over the little town. I wonder how they will ever get to the summit.

It's raining when Suzanne starts her five-day climb. From the covered walkway, I sit and watch droplets, like sparkling beads, form in neat rows on the undersides of plant leaves. As puddles form around me, I wonder how she and her group are doing. On this day, fog obscures the mountain. But I know it's there.

After breakfast Juma and Elia, another waiter, invite me to accompany them to the local orphanage. Suzanne and I had read that it's a good idea to bring candy and pens for the orphans so I bring them with me on this first volunteer day. Outside the hotel gates, the town changes dramatically— muddy dirt roads, meager cement houses, a chicken running around clucking, a young barefoot boy crying. The orphanage itself is bright and cheery with colorful painted walls and new playground equipment.

I do a little team teaching with the waiters. The students, all looking to be under 10 years old, are learning English today—lucky for me! And they capture my hearts immediately as they repeat words we are practicing. I add a little movement demonstration for "up" and "down" by bending down and reaching up. The class, tightly packed at long tables, follows along, enjoying the repetitive movement. Later we go outside to the playground, where I get some hugs and watch them frolic freely. A few girls start to braid my hair. Helping and giving bring great joy, but there's a sadness too. This is an orphanage. I imagine each child's difficult story.

I decide to ditch a day trip to the waterfall and spend the money on some food for the children. Juma and Elia take me on the hotel shuttle bus to the bustling markets. Tailors stitching garments line the roadside with their ancient foot-pumping sewing machines. Since I am in town for five days, I want to do as the Tanzanians do and wear an authentic skirt. So, our first stop will be at a fabric shop where I choose a bright blue material with a yellow and red pattern. Next we visit their favorite tailor, who licketty split, creates a brilliant wrap around skirt that I will wear on my other volunteer days.

At the market I meet Juma's mother, a tomato seller, surrounded by a dazzling assortment of brightly colored fresh fruits and vegetables. The guys help me choose the best rice and oil for the orphanage. For 100 bucks, we get a giant bag that will last five months and oil that will last about nine months. Juma and Elia smell each bag of rice to ensure its quality, and at the last moment, just before paying, they switch it for a better bag.

The next day at the orphanage, this time in my new blue skirt, they have some kitchen work for me — sifting through the rice for impurities. We swirl the grains around in round baskets, picking out anything that doesn't look like it belongs. I finish up the morning outside playing hand games and doing puzzles with the kids. It is sweet how they just adapt to my presence.

In the afternoons I cool off in the hotel pool, read, and write. Other climbers come and go. There are several routes and the trips run concurrently. At meals I become the resident listener for the ones who return with success stories and others who share their struggles. Not everyone completes the journey. Of course I am curious about Suzanne.

An entire group returns before they reach the summit because of heavy rains. The last leg of the trail is slippery and they are soaked and muddy. *Hmmm wonder how Suzanne's group is doing.* Another day a British hiker is brought down on a stretcher when his knee gives out. A German woman from Suzanne's group experiences painful nosebleeds, so she and her husband come down early. And an American ex-pat living in Norway gets altitude sickness and cannot hold down any food or water. In retrospect, he tells me, he would have taken longer breaks and slowed his pace. Slow and steady, with patience, is the way to a successful trek, I am told.

Did you see my daughter? I ask everyone who comes down from the mountain. And there is always news of Suzanne. She is standing on her head on the mountain. She is smiling. She is encouraging others. She is the Suzanne that I know and love.

Two Canadians, who have successfully finished their trek, will be heading home soon. One of the pair, Dan, has lost his wife to cancer and is traveling around the world to the places they wanted to go to together. Kilimanjaro is his last stop. His friend Ryan is there for support. I like these two. Dan shows me their wedding photo taken in the hospital ten days before his wife died. They invite me to join them for a shopping excursion. And Ryan treats us to lunch at an Indian restaurant. This part of town with souvenir shops is pretty empty and the merchants spot us tourists almost immediately. I am followed by a young man who wants me to buy some of his artwork, which I finally do for five bucks. Ryan is looking for a specific bowl and as he goes from store to store, a small group of merchants gather around him competing for his business. They all talk at once in English and Swahili, each one offering the "best" bargain or deal. As their volume crescendos, the confusion intensifies. Without thinking, I do a weird flapping motion with my arms, like I am a frightened pelican, and this gets everybody to calm down. After a stunned moment, laughter breaks out. And while Ryan steps into a shop, the locals stand outside on the porch and chat with me about their beloved President Obama and Mama Clinton.

Finally, it's summit day for Suzanne. No one mentions it by name—Kilimanjaro. They just call it "the mountain." At 19, 341 feet, it is the highest freestanding mountain in the world. From a spot just outside my hotel room, I can see it in the distance as the clouds have dispersed and the sky is blue again. The night before, a full moon revealed a sky full of stars. I think Suzanne chose these particular dates for her climb based on the full moon, for extra light. And the weather has cooperated. She thinks of everything!

It is not surprising to me that she makes it to the top, just slightly delirious. For the last stretch there is unexpected wind, which makes it challenging, but she does it! She later tells me that in her mind, she is heading towards the hotel, and not the summit. Altitude can trick the mind. Good thing she really wanted to get to the hotel!

The driver invites me to go with him to meet her at the ending point at 3,000 ft. I am thrilled to see her looking so exhuberent. Back at the hotel she has a couple of Kilimanjaro beers with the other climbers and photos are taken. At a ceremony, certificates are presented. I am a proud Momma.

CHAPTER 16

Sweet Safari

After the thrill of climbing Mt. Kilimanjaro, it is a bit anti-climactic for Suzanne when we embark on our four-day safari. Soon after bonding with our lively, charming driver Joseph, we learn that he will be with us only until the first gas station, about an hour outside of Moshi.

While waiting there for our new driver, I figure it's a good time to use the "toilet" at the back of the station. I open the door to a hole in the cement floor. That's it. I stand there for a minute, staring at the hole and figuring out how best to maneuver. So what do I decide? I get completely undressed. Getting urine on my clothing is not how I envision the safari's beginning. Lucky for us, this is the most challenging of the "facilities," because we are mostly glamping.

Suz is recuperating from the climb and dozes, but perks up when families of baboons appear, blocking the road. Dozens of them. On our first day, we also see elephant families and herds of zebras, buffalo, wildebeests, giraffes, and more. They surround our Jeep. Did you know that baby zebras have brown stripes, not black? A teenage elephant taking a bath splashes at the edge of a lake. I think I see him smile. It is their world and we are just visiting it. Being in this landscape sends chills of excitement through my body. Even Suzanne, exhausted from the trek, feels the energy.

We are the only two in our vehicle—a semi-private experience just by luck. Our new driver Arthur is knowledgable but doesn't talk much. After 20 years of driving, he has lost count of the number of safaris he's been on. His formality, stiffness, and lack of smiles is jolting after the easy rhythms of Joseph. Suzanne and I steal glances at each other, raising an eyebrow to communicate our concern for how the mood of the trip will be.

As it turns out, Arthur is a true professional. He gets the job done, transporting us to flush toilets, meals, hotels, and our glamp sites.

Suzanne labels his driving *aggressive*, based on the evidence that he nearly hits a zebra and some goats, and doesn't seem to care much about the local wandering dogs or the migrating wildebeests crossing the road. On the way from the Negorongoro Crater to the Serengeti National Park, we come to an abrupt halt facing a flooded road. Safari vehicles are lined up on both sides of this giant puddle, more like a small lake, formed by the previous day's downpour. The drivers are wondering if they should take the chance of ruining their vehicles by moving through it. Suzanne predicts that Arthur will be first.

After 45 minutes in the hot, unforgiving sun, a big truck arrives and just goes for it. The other drivers assess the depth by watching cautiously, but it is our Arthur who plows through the giant puddle first, exactly as Suzanne expected. She gets a high five for that!

Turns out that Arthur's bland personality does not affect his ability to spot the wildlife. Spotting wildlife is his forte. In the Serengeti we see a rare cheetah and some hyenas. There are lions everywhere. In the grass we see a male walking, then two females. Arthur finds a mother lion nursing her cubs, which reminds me of the sweetness of nursing my daughters. And he spots nine lions sleeping in an umbrella acacia tree—a tree dripping lions! A half dozen vehicles have surrounded this tree, a popular spot for viewing. Some noisy tourists begin to climb on the front of their vehicle for a better look. Arthur doesn't appear to have a high regard for them. "So rude," he mutters. A few of the lions wake up and think the same thing. But, their bellies are full and they are sleepy. And they would not like the taste of humans anyway, especially rude ones! As we drive away we see a family of hippos in a pool making burping noises and yawning.

In the back seat Suz and I have some laughs. It is an understatement to say that my skills at spotting wildlife are not on par with our guide's. What I think is an animal, is often a rock or a tree branch. Suzanne finds this hilarious and teases me. I am keeping a list of every animal or plant that is found and named. The lilac-breasted roller, a bird native to the African savanna, fascinates me, but I say *roasted* instead of *breasted* and Suzanne can't stop laughing. Finally relaxed and rested from her trek, Suzanne becomes giddier by the minute. My mistakes set her off on waves of deep belly-laughs which are contagious. We laugh until tears roll down our faces. The memory still makes me giggle.

Every time we see warthogs, we sing the line from "Hakuna Matada" in *The Lion King,* "When I was a young warthoog." Our guide Arthur pronounces the word with the th sound so it comes out *war-thog.* Suzanne and I find this hysterical every time he says it, which is often, because they are everywhere. We have become the unruly kids in the back seat with stern Dad Arthur driving us. We are the hippos in the pool, burping and yawning, the teenage elephant splashing. Maybe it is the seriousness of Arthur that helps bring out our sillies.

Arthur comes through for us again when we are driving through the Ngorongor Crater, a caldera, an erupted volcano that fell into itself. The grasses fed by the nutrient-rich volcanic soil are the brightest of greens here and the animals love it. He parks the Jeep on the road in the middle of a giant herd of wildebeests who are munching peacefully on their nutritious lunch. In the distance, far beyond the herd, Arthur spots a rare black rhino grazing solo. He hands us his binoculars so we can share in the moment.

Suddenly, there is a hush in the herd. Ngorongoro is already a quiet place, but now it is completely silent. We have been so thrilled with the black rhino spotting that we don't notice when a lioness begins to meander through the herd. The silence alerts us. The wildebeests don't want to draw any attention to themselves, just in case she's hungry. They don't run and they don't fight. They freeze. Lucky for the wildebeests that day, the lioness is full and taking an after dinner stroll. As the threat leaves, we hear again the ripping of grass, the movement of jaws, and the chewing of teeth. With a big exhale, Suzanne and I enjoy this peaceful moment.

With his trusty binoculars, Arthur spots a group of lions feeding on a buffalo in another spot in the Crater. Again, he shares the binoculars with us and I'm relieved that we don't see this close up. Even if it is the natural thing, it is still hard to watch.

I'm grateful for this time with Suzanne and thankful that none of her friends wanted to go. But my feelings are mixed. I'm sad for this to end, and I don't know what awaits her in Dallas, now that her training focus has finished. And I have no control over what comes next. We embrace and say our goodbyes in the Philadelphia airport where her connecting flight leaves right away. And as she turns away from me to go, I cry.

CHAPTER 17

Texas Revisited

Six months after the Tanzania trip, Suzanne's marriage ends. Somewhere in that time period, she concludes that they don't want the same things. Getting a divorce in Texas is easy, but divorce is divorce—a major life decision and change that is stressful. She moves to a new apartment and throws herself into rock climbing.

Just a few months later, in the fall of 2016, I'm excited when she invites me to visit and convinces me to try top-rope climbing at the climbing gym. She informs me that she has a new rock-climbing boyfriend and she wants me to meet him.

Top-rope climbing? Who am I kidding? I'd much rather have my feet planted on solid ground. But I have agreed to do this thing for Suzanne, because it will make her happy and I am all about getting out of my comfort zone and trying new things. I mean, she isn't asking me to parachute jump out of a plane, although she's done it. For me that would be a hard NO.

I *assess* the situation. There are lots of mats everywhere and they are pretty thick, good for a soft landing, I think. And all sorts of people (even children) are climbing everywhere on all kinds of courses. The climbs are arranged by level of difficulty, so mine is the first one, right near the main desk and the door. I assume it is arranged this way in case of broken bones or sprains. The important people would spot a problem and get the injured person (maybe me) out in an ambulance as fast as possible.

I can feel my throat tighten and my mouth dry up. Where is that water bottle? My belly tenses as I am presented with the special shoes that help you stick better. There is a brief training by an official person, and I step into the harness. The new boyfriend comes over to give me some tips. He is an experienced climber and easy on the eyes. I can see why Suzanne likes him.

The way this works is you have a partner—you are not on your own. Suzanne is mine. We are literally attached by hooks with ropes. It is the first time we have been physically attached since those early days of the umbilical cord. We are responsible for making sure the other gets down safely. Trust is the essential ingredient. Suzanne seems excited and alert.

I am so very kind to let her go first. I become the *belayer* for her. She flies up the novice climb with her sticky shoes in like a minute while I let out the rope little by little until she gets up. Then I do all the right things to let her down without damage, breathing a sigh of relief that I don't kill her. I make her landing pleasant and comfortable. This ability to do something so direct and connected to my daughter is delicious. Since she moved from Philly and since the Africa trip, I have longed for a deeper connection. I am not bad at belaying. So, we do it again.

Then, my turn. Suzanne takes charge of the ropes and I begin the ascent. I grab onto the little holds sticking out from the walls. They are different colors and shapes and my artist eye enjoys the visual. I place a foot on one, and grab another with my hand. Suzanne is giving me suggestions for placement. It becomes like a dance: a hand—breathe, a foot—breathe, a hand—breathe, a foot—breathe. The breathing is essential to the process. Arm and leg strength makes it possible to get to the next colored hold. I begin to relax a little and breathe easier as I realize that all the yoga and dance I've done over the years has made me flexible and strong. I am in the moment thinking only about my next move.

I can see why Suzanne enjoys this, with everything she is going through. Climbing this way occupies the brain and prevents you from worrying about anything else except the next move. So, bit by bit, I make my way up. Eventually I get to the top. Success. I've made it! Now what?

Unfortunately, the descent is an entirely different experience. In the ascent, I am fighting against gravity. Now it wants to take me fast to those thick, soft mats below. Getting there requires letting go—removing my hands and feet that have been placed solidly on those lovely multi-colored holds. Although it feels to me like I am on top of the Empire State Building, it's maybe 30 feet.

I look down at Suzanne. I wait. Letting go is really hard. I have let go of so many things in my life: my marriage, my teaching job, my younger daughter. Now, all I have to do is free my hands and feet from the wall and trust my daughter to help me. There have been so many years when I couldn't count on her, when she was heavily using drugs and alcohol. There were times when I didn't know where she was or what she was doing.

I don't want to do it. I stay up there for a while. Deciding. But there is no other way down. Suzanne is drinking again. But not at this moment. And she is there waiting.

"I got you, Mom," she says and I believe her. I trust her. Even with all the ups and downs we have been through over the years, I know she loves and cares about me. I don't remember her ever uttering those exact words. "I got you, Mom." I take a few deep breaths. And then I do it. I let go. A little like coming down a roller coaster hill but a lot slower. I have relinquished control and my belayer, Suzanne, gets me down. I am in free fall, but I am attached to my daughter.

With Suzanne's help, and a few kicks on the wall, I am lowered to the mat. I am so relieved that I'm down. And even though there is exhilaration from the accomplishment, and gratitude for the trust, I don't need to do this again.

I don't know then how much more I will have to let go of in the future.

CHAPTER 18

On the Road Again

March, 2017

Six months later, I fly out for what will be our "Mother /daughter roadtrip from Dallas to Denver," where Suzanne decides to make another fresh start. I'm hoping my presence and support can help to lighten things up.

Dallas hadn't been going well.

When she hung a dress on the sprinkler system spout, her new apartment flooded. She had to stay in a motel for a week and a lot of possessions got ruined. When I visited her afterward, we went shopping for new home items to brighten the place, but that didn't seem to lift her mood.

Then she got into a frustrating fender-bender that required car repairs. Luckily she had excellent insurance for both. The divorce plus these events have a cumulative affect and she is suffering—more than she lets on.

In the middle of the gloom, she participates in a fulfilling medical mission to Mexico, where helping others lifts her spirits. There's also the new boyfriend from the climbing gym. Life stuff, good and bad, but Suzanne can't seem to shake the heaviness.

Part of the frustration with Dallas is her job. Although she had enjoyed the medical mission, she wasn't crazy about the "culture" in her hospital. It's an old boys' club, unfriendly to women—completely different from Philadelphia. There's a good chance Denver will be more progressive, she hopes.

Denver, with its majestic peaks and endless rock-climbing opportunities, beckons. It's a place she had always wanted to go—because of the Rockies, she tells me. I didn't remember that she had applied to nursing school there.

With the help of Emilie and Brian, Philly friends living in Denver, she finds an apartment and a job as a nurse anesthetist in an eye clinic, similar to the position in Philly at the Wills Eye Center. There's hope.

By the time I arrive in Dallas, much has been done. The climbing-gym boyfriend had been assisting with the initial moving and packing the "cube," which is already in transit and will arrive in Denver after we do. They assign me some cleaning, but mostly I'm dog sitting my granddog, which is really like dog entertainment because Mully and his new girlfriend, the boyfriend's German Shepard Ginger, have become the best of friends. I get to watch them snuggle. These two will definitely miss each other.

As Suzanne and her boyfriend continue their rhythmic riding up and down the elevator, loading up the car, he talks about moving to Denver. Silence from Suzanne. I can see that she is exhausted. The boyfriend might be high. Their conversation is abrupt and strained. "I'm sick of his freeloading," Suzanne whispers to me, after he heads out into the hallway.

Initially I had thought that he was good for her, but I find out later that he has his own issues around substances. I wonder if Suzanne is doing more than drinking. I'm here to be supportive in any way that's needed.

Road trip day is overcast and gloomy. The three of us go out for lunch and Suzanne downs a giant glass of beer before she says her good-byes to the boyfriend and gets behind the wheel of the car. It is against my better judgment, but I decide not to make waves. However, I cautiously observe how she drives, and she seems okay. We split the 12-hour drive, into two days and share the driving. She and the boyfriend continue their fight via text, which Suzanne can speak out loud into her phone, so I have a front row seat for the event. An hour later, she finally admits that the alcohol and exhaustion have caught up with her and she needs to rest.

Relieved to take over, I find a country music station to listen to while she sleeps besides me. Also sleeping is her precious Mully in a small spot on the back seat which is stuffed to the brim with her things. All is quiet.

While they rest, I take in the scenery. There's not much variety in the miles and miles of flat and mostly barren Texas panhandle. With hardly any traffic, my breathing slows and the muscles of my shoulders let go. Some wind farms flash by. A giant herd of cows grazes on the pale grasses. On my right, a freight train moves parallel to the highway. The pallet of this locale is shades of beige, grey, and yellow ochre. So much sky. I waver between moments of peace and nagging worry. *How will she do in this new place? Will a change of locale brighten her spirits?* There have been so many fresh starts.

Amarillo, Texas is the midway point and we find a motel. After just a short pit stop along the way, Mully is thrilled to be out of the car. Suzanne is too exhausted so I volunteer to take him out for a much-needed walk. When we return to the room, he shows his playful exuberance as he springs back and forth, like a Slinky, between the motel beds. Even though Suzanne can hardly move, she finds this funny. So do I. I get to hear her laugh, courtesy of our goofy Mully.

The next morning I take the first shift which passes through New Mexico. As we enter Colorado, the majestic Rocky Mountains loom over the prairie like a giant fortress of stone and snow. I have never seen them this way and I'm trying to salvage a bit of joy from this road trip. When I attempt to rouse Suzanne so she can also enjoy the moment, she opens one eye, takes a peek and is not impressed. She mutters something like, *no big deal,* and falls back into slumber, so I marvel at their awesomeness all on my own, but wish she could share this moment with me.

She takes the last shift as we come into the Denver city limits—back into civilization, noise, and traffic. Her new place is a sleek and modern high-rise right smack in the middle of the city. From her bedroom window, you can see the mountains and I am way more excited about this than she is. It's lovely and there's lots of sun, but no furniture. We sleep on an air mattress on her floor that night.

The next day we purchase a new couch and a bed which she will need help assembling when it is delivered. The pod/cube will be arriving in a few days, so she will have a lot of work to do after I leave, but she has her friends Emilie and Brian who have offered to help. She is not totally alone. With her friends here and all that climbing ahead of her, I feel hopeful that this new start will be a good one.

Later when she drives me to the airport, she realizes that the gas tank is almost empty. We drive in uncomfortable silence all over the airport looking for gas and the stress is palpable as my gut tightens. We don't know if I will make my flight or if she will have enough gas to get back home. Eventually, we find a gas station, but Suzanne's mood is still gloomy. Is she regretting volunteering to drive me? Is she angry for not being aware of the gas gauge before we set out? Maybe it's the task of moving that she finds daunting. Moving to a new place—again. I think back to our giggly safari ride. Was that just a year ago?. How things have changed. And I get out of the car with a very unsettled feeling.

CHAPTER 19

Rocky Mountain Low

Mothers' Day, 2017

Two months later, my mom and I fly to Denver to visit Suzanne for Mother's Day weekend. This will be the last time we see her alive. My mother hadn't spent any significant time with Suzanne in two years, and I still haven't told her about the relapse. It's been almost three years since she started drinking. And it's not getting better. I still hope that she will reach out for help, when she is ready, like she has done before.

Grandma is a worrier. About everything. Her concerns about Suzanne are not without merit. Most of our conversations these last few years have been about how Suzanne was doing and how frustrated we were that we couldn't do anything about it. I had decided to spare my mother additional worry about the relapse. She had already lost one grandchild.

We're meeting Suzanne at the end of her work day, so Mom and I have a little time to kill. We have a pleasant lunch in a local restaurant, which my mother will later describe as the most relaxing part of the trip.

As soon as we arrive at Suzanne's apartment, I sense a weird energy. We haven't all been together since she left Philly, although I've seen her every couple of months. Our rhythms are off. We can't seem to figure out what to do next, stumbling over words to avoid confrontation. At one point, I say something like, *Isn't it sweet how much we all love each other, that we want to make sure we are all pleased?* The truth is, it's awkward.

Mostly, Suzanne wants us to see her climb. She seems more than excited about sharing this with us. Mom and I exchange a look as she goes on and on talking incessantly about the climbing options. One is a rocky area just off the side of a road, she tells us, but that's a bit of a drive and Mom and I are tired from the long flight and not that outdoorsy. We didn't even pack sneakers. And we're not scheduled to pick up mom's rented wheelchair until the next day. We settle on the climbing gym. It's not that she just *wants* to be climbing on something somewhere—she *needs* to.

I take photos and videos of her graceful ascent to the top of the wall at the gym. Other photos show the three of us with linked arms that look normal and happy, but there is an undercurrent of strain.

Afterwards, at dinner in a Greek restaurant, a brand new boyfriend joins us. They have had only a few dates and it might be a bit early to meet the family, I think. Conversation is lively and he doesn't have any problem letting Suzanne pay for the meal. I make a mental note that he doesn't even offer. We had talked about Suz staying with us that night, but the hotel doesn't accept dogs. She ends up staying at her place with the ungenerous boyfriend.

In the morning when she doesn't call us at the agreed time, Mom and I wait in the hotel lobby. Although my gut tightens, I try to reassure my mother that everything is okay. Eventually, when we hear from Suzanne, she sounds tired and out of sorts. She tells me that the boyfriend broke up with her. "Oh, Suz. I'm sorry," I tell her. "We can talk about it later if you want." Silence.

Suzanne has been so unpredictable in her moods, we don't know which Suzanne we will see at breakfast. I do know that she is doing her best to show us a good time, even with this latest curveball in her life.

There is some extended uncomfortable silence during eggs and bacon at the Denver Diner. While chewing, Mom decides that this is the perfect moment to blurt out, "You know, Suzanne, your biological clock is ticking." Silence. *Shit, here we go.* Even though there has always been unconditional love and acceptance between Suzanne and her grandma, I am worried about Suzanne's reaction to the timing of this statement.

Suzanne puts her fork down. We all do the same.

Mom is telling Suzanne to hurry up and get married so she can have great-grandchildren. I get it. In her mind, she has done nothing wrong. She's almost 90 and we should be used to her bluntness. Over the years, Suzanne has always given her a pass, while I have been the one upset by these sorts of comments. "Grandma, you can say anything," Suzanne would tell her, usually while wrapping her arms around her. Grandma, in return, accepted Suzanne unconditionally. Always. In her eyes, she could do no wrong. I have been the one left out of this relationship, and had vowed never to come between them.

But this time is different. It feels more like a cockfight, with neither side giving in.

Suzanne gives her grandmother an icy look, a scowl, in fact. She is clearly upset, vulnerable, and angry with my mother's assessment of her egg viability. And there is something else going on that we can't put our fingers on.

Then, Suzanne jumps up from the booth and flies out of the diner.

"I don't know why she's so upset," my mother says as she adjusts her scarf and sits up straight.

"I mean, did you really have to bring that up now? You know that guy just broke up with her." I take a deep breath and I look her in the eye. "You should apologize."

"I don't think so. I didn't say anything wrong."

Clearly, I am not making headway with my mother, so I go outside to find my daughter. Suzanne is leaning against the car, smoking a cigarette from her secret emergency stash in the glove box. I don't make any excuses for my mother. "Grandma shouldn't have said that," I offer. She takes another deep drag of the cigarette and blows the smoke out slowly. "I'll be okay," she says. 'Give me a minute." I hug her and kiss her on the cheek, and go back into the diner, though I am not convinced she is okay.

I've put myself right in the middle this time and I'm not sure if there's anything that I can say or do that will mend this rift. My mother can't understand what she has done wrong. She won't apologize, although I continue to encourage her. Suzanne eventually composes herself. We all pretend it didn't happen, and end up having a lovely day.

Suzanne had planned a stop at a local casino, my mom's favorite thing, and we have some laughs there, because Suz and I are not gamblers. We walk on a nature trail, pushing Mom in the wheelchair. Afterward, we drive up to Boulder for dinner at a global eatery, where at an even higher altitude than Denver, I end up with Afib while sipping a cocktail. Suzanne makes a bold move and orders a gin and tonic. This is the first time Grandma sees her drink. My mom and I exchange a sideways look. This time Mom doesn't say anything. Perhaps, after the breakfast fiasco, she thinks she has said enough. Better to keep the peace now.

On this same day, one of her best friends, Becca, is in town and Suzanne had arranged to see her later that night. I volunteer to sleep at the apartment with Mully so she can spend the night at the hotel with my Mom. By the end of the day she is exhausted. She cancels the get-together with Becca and goes home. *Why is she so tired? Why doesn't she want to see her friend? What's going on in her head?*

The next day before we go home, we have a wild, windy Jeep ride at the Garden of the Gods in Colorado Springs. We've put Mom in the front where she feels very important and can ask the driver lots of questions about these unusual rock formations all around us. Also there she won't get car sick. Suz and I are happy to take the back seat where there are blankets and snacks. We've brought along Mully, who cuddles with us under the blankets as we are jostled about on the bumpy ride with our hair blowing all over our faces. Suzanne's eyes are hidden behind dark sunglasses. *What are you hiding? Are you sad?* During this brief moment of fun, she still seems deflated. We are all pretending a little.

After lunch in downtown Colorado Springs, we take a stroll, Mom walking Mully from the wheelchair. The mountain air is clean and fresh. When we pass a cannabis dispensary, Suzanne encourages us to stop and take some photos, for a laugh, but I don't find it funny. Recreational marijuana is legal here and I'm pretty sure she has already partaken. For a person with addictions, this is not necessarily a good thing. *Are there other substances added to the mix?*

Her strong level of interest in this shop sends warning signs to my gut which tightens as I remembered that she had encouraged me to visit one the last time I was there. We live so far apart now, and my adult daughter is making choices that I can't control.

"Is Suzanne bi-polar?" my mother wonders the next morning as we pack up at the hotel. Both of us observed her ups and downs that weekend. My mother has had the most distance from Suzanne, so maybe she has the clearest view. I wonder about that too and spend a lot of time thinking about it on the plane ride home.

We never get to find out.

PART II
After

CHAPTER 20

Homecoming, September, 2017

The two suitcases and I make it back to Philly, just a week since the death of my daughter. Somehow my body knows how to get me out of bed even though sleep is elusive. I eat and drink water and even make my bed. The ancient part of my brain takes over and accomplishes tasks, while the rest of me is numb. My mantra for moving forward is, *I will just do the next thing I have to do,* and after that task is completed, I say it again. And again.

From my carry-on suitcase, I gingerly remove the box of ashes and place it on the floor of my walk-in closet below the blouses and besides my dance shoes. I know that Suzanne's spirit is not in the ashes.

From Suzanne's suitcase I remove items taken from her apartment. The green measuring spoon and the dragonfly dish end up on the kitchen counter next to the stove, where I will use them when I prepare morning tea. The measuring spoon, a teaspoon, is exactly the amount I need for a cup of green tea. I scoop the dried leaves out of a pouch, pour them into the pot, and return the spoon to the little dragonfly dish, while I wait for the water to boil. My body remembers how to boil water. But now Suzanne's presence is with me.

I place her make-up brushes in my stainless steel utility cup on the bathroom sink. Each morning Suzanne's brush will touch my face with a light pink blush. From her face to mine. The SEPTA tokens and jewelry will go in a new silver box. I put the remaining items: paperwork, computer, phone, and journals on the floor in neat piles. This will be my work moving forward.

The journals and the phone scare me because they contain proof that Suzanne was angry with me and not just me, but also her dad and her current boyfriend. At the very end, her last entries show that she was not angry with everyone. There are compliments and loving words written about some of her friends and her grandma. But not about me.

Suicide notes are overrated.

So, I open the journals and close them right away. I easily get into the phone using Lisa's birthday as the passcode and see a flurry of desperate texts she wrote to the boyfriend, as he was breaking up with her. I shut down the phone. My head hurts and there's a dagger in my gut. It is all too much.

There is a memorial to organize. I wait a full month to have it because everyone is in shock, including me. Researching suicide, reading everything I can find, I try to understand it, if that's possible. Then, I will speak about it at the memorial. The Alliance of Hope website, an online support group for suicide loss, provides a lifeline in the early days. I grab onto anything I can learn that helps me get to the next day.

The memorial will be at the Unitarian Church, a few blocks away from my apartment. Although I am not Unitarian, not a practicing anything, I am spiritual. This place seems open and welcoming. Suzanne and I once attended an event there. I think she would like it. Suzanne's best friend Lauren offers to gather photographs from various stages of her life and frame them to be displayed at the back of the church.

✳ ✳ ✳

When I return to work, just a few days after the trip to Denver, I enter into deep silence with people who don't know me well and don't know what's happened. To hold it together, I avoid eye contact. I distract myself with books and crossword puzzles on my breaks, so I don't burst into tears. Others may think I am unfriendly, but it's simply survival.

What does a mother do when her daughter dies before their relationship is mended? What happens when the ending is bad and the daughter goes out hating the mother?

What do you do with that?

It's hard enough even when the relationship is good.

"I have a healthy relationship with a person on the Other Side," That's what I have been saying about Lisa in the seventeen years since she's been gone. With Lisa, there were no loose ends. It was an accident and I never took on any guilt or shame. There was anger that it happened and plenty of sadness. Uncomplicated sadness. Deep uncomplicated sadness that had me crying anywhere and everywhere for years, but no guilt.

After Lisa's passing, I started seeing dragonflies everywhere. Some Native Americans believe that the dragonfly represents the soul of the departed. Lisa is with me. There was never a doubt that she was okay in her energy form and perfect in the non-physical realm.

Suzanne's passing is different. She goes out angry and deep in her addiction. Part of her anger is directed at me, but I take all of it. I'm her mother, dammit. Tears do not come easily because of the many other conflicting emotions that I didn't have after Lisa died: fear, guilt, remorse, and shame. I believe it is all my fault and I have to live with that.

I also possess a weird belief that since I have already lost a child, I'm some kind of a grief expert and because of that, Suzanne's death will be easier to process. That's stupid. Obviously, I'm in shock and out of my mind. It's like saying having another child will replace the one you lost. I do know for sure in my deepest inner being that eventually I will feel better and when I do, I will have the relationship with Suzanne that I want.

However, I don't know when that will happen or what I will have to go through along the way.

CHAPTER 21

The Memorial

In the drab beige Macy's dressing room, three droopy faces look back at me. I have seen this person before, but not for a while. I see my half-dressed figure in various angles from the trio of adjoining mirrors. On the walls are a few black scuff marks, as if someone had scraped a shoe here and there. Three dark dresses hang from the rack and I am studying them, trying to decide which one I will wear for my daughter's memorial. They all fit me. My eyes move from the faces in the mirror back to the dresses. There is no time to dwell on my appearance. I will speak at Suzanne's memorial and share her life. No parent ever wants to buy a dress for this reason.

I decide on a tailored short sleeved number, in a dark navy with tiny white dots. This will be the only time I wear it. I know that because I have been through this before.

Lisa's graduation from the Family School, was just a few months before the accident. A joyful celebration, we had a grand and giddy time posing for photos—back to back in one, and in each other's arms for another. The golden sun illuminated our smiles. This was a perfect day. Both girls were alive and their futures were ahead of them.

At Lisa's funeral, I wanted to bring in some of the positive energy of her graduation day, so I wore the same outfit from the photos—a long black skirt with a light brown top. Afterward, the skirt and top remained untouched in my closet for a couple of years before I decided to let them go to Goodwill. I couldn't put on the same clothes that I had worn for my daughter's funeral. It was too heavy.

I know it will be the same this time.

On the outside, I appear quite normal, but there is a sharp dagger in my gut that no one can see.

Dressed in the smart never-to-be-worn-again Macy's dress I stand at the podium of the Unitarian church looking out at the faces of family and friends. As I read my prepared speech my voice sounds unfamiliar as it bellows from the microphone. It is a hot September afternoon and the back doors are open. Perhaps people on the street can hear me.

Without knowing anything about "safe" and "effective" messaging at the time, I intuitively know that it's not a good idea to share the specific details of Suzanne's suicide. For a vulnerable person in the audience, it could be triggering. I also don't talk about her addiction.

When I say "There is no shame," I can feel the words in the moment, but I haven't embodied them, as I am in shock. For now, these words are a goal, a promise. A *fake it 'til you make it* experience, as much for me as for those listening. I sense a huge energy field behind me, holding me up and giving me strength to speak without faltering. I do it for Suzanne and with Suzanne. It is as if, in that moment, all the ancestors have gathered to support me.

I want everyone to know about Suzanne so I tell some stories from the past. So do her friends, as they are invited to get up one by one. I tell the story of the plum. We laugh and cry, as we did at Lisa's funeral. There are musical performances and a playlist of spiritual and healing music that I have carefully selected.

And for the end, there's a special plan, inspired by Suzanne. I have told a few of Suzanne's closest friends to just "go with me." When I give Lauren the signal, she runs to the back room, turns on the dance music, and cranks up the volume. And I invite everyone to come up and dance. Many join in, so we shake it out and shake it off, at least for the moment. And I know that Suzanne approves.

I am told that my words help some friends and family, but I know underneath it all, everyone, including me, is still thinking about the way she died. How can you not? I wanted the day to celebrate the best of Suzanne with stories, photographs, music, and dancing and it did.

CHAPTER 22

The Apology Tour

On the outside I appear to function as a human as I show myself to the world, but inside, I am anxious and confused. Everyone who was close to Suzanne, including me, is on a quest to figure things out. The elusive "Why?" is on our minds. We all have some guilt, thinking we could have or should have done more.

The little pieces of information baffle us as we try to put them together like a puzzle. Only the pieces don't fit. And our brains, deep in grief, have trouble processing. We are not inside Suzanne's brain at the end. She had distanced herself from all of us one by one, and confided only certain things to certain people. She divied out her life in bits, so that no one had a complete picture. We learn after some time that we will never truly know the why, but it keeps us busy.

I go back into her journals. The one with the "suicide note," covers her five months in Denver. The other has a couple of entries written in Dallas from November, 2016 through January, 2017. In this earlier one, she says lovely things about me, and I appear on a few of her gratitude lists, but that changes drastically by the end of the second journal.

Reading descriptions of her anger and mental struggles at the end devastates me. It consumes me. It adds to my guilt and remorse. And I don't know what to do.

So I begin apologizing.

The first time is right after I learn about her passing. I do a guided meditation and at the end, all I want to do is say I'm sorry for not being able to help her and save her. So I say it again and again.

I'm sorry. I'm sorry. I'm sorry…..

I find myself walking down the street and a thought or memory pops in my head of something I regret. I say out loud on busy Market Street, "That was stupid,"as people pass me by. And "That was stupid," comes out of my mouth another day on Walnut Street. Same on Chestnut Street and possibly every street I've walked on in Center City. Sometimes I literally have to stop and collect myself because the jolt of a memory is so intense. Did I really say that or do that? It's the walking apology tour covering the entirety of the 37 years I have Suzanne on this planet. And after each realization, I apologize. And continue walking.

I know that in order to get to that healthy relationship, with a person on the Other Side, who happens to be my daughter, there has to be forgiveness. And although I am a little angry that she didn't ask for help this time, it is easy for me to forgive Suzanne. She had mental and addiction struggles. Forgiving myself is the hard part. And it will be the key part to having the relationship that I long for.

CHAPTER 23

Traveling With Ashes

December, 2017

Some of Suzanne's ashes are traveling with me in my suitcase, this time in a plastic baggie secured with rubber bands. I've scooped them out of the box which still remains on my walk-in closet floor. I am headed by bus and train to the Berkshires to get some rest and rejuvenate at Kripalu, where freshly fallen snow has completely covered the grounds. Picture perfect New England snow, unspoiled by cars, trucks, and people—and I can't wait to walk in it. I welcome this break from the noise and fast pace of the city.

The first morning there, after an early breakfast, I venture out with the baggie in my coat pocket. My footprints will be first in the new snow. I find a stick and draw "SUZ" in the snow, then sprinkle in some of her ashes. I am flooded with memories of Suzanne and me at Kripalu. I miss her. The next day it snows again and covers up her name, so I draw it again. I know her ashes are somewhere under the snow and when spring comes and the melting starts, those ashes will be mixed with the earth of the Berkshire Mountains.

At Kripalu I do yoga and practice meditation, tools that helped me greatly after Lisa died. I also begin to write like crazy. *Finally, it's time to start writing some books.* I feel like writing will help me sort things out.

The ashes make the rounds in the first year after her passing. I parcel them out to friends who take them to Japan, Pike's Peak, and a Hawaiian mountain top. I hope Suzanne will enjoy, if enjoyment is a thing in heaven, knowing that her ashes have been scattered on mountain tops. I've heard that on the Other Side, they don't give a whit about what we do for their funeral and memorials. It only needs to make us happy, serving the living in some way. On the Other Side, it is not important.

A few weeks later, some of Suzanne's ashes accompany me to Playa Zicatela, on the west coast of Mexico. The trip was booked months before she died. I never got around to inviting her to join me and share my little bungalow, as I had planned. She was so angry with me at the time. I thought, *I don't want to have her with me if she is so angry.* Something else to regret. *What if I had invited her?. Would that have changed anything?*

As soon as I step into my bungalow, I am surprised by a phone call from Vincent, the ex-boyfriend. I hadn't spoken with him since the airport. I put down my suitcase to take the call. It is late December and he wants to wish me a happy new year. "You're going to have a great year," he tells me. What an idiot!

I suppose I could have said, "Well I can't lose any more daughters!" But it was awkward enough already.

The sun's warmth and the ocean provides some healing almost immediately, when I scatter Suzanne's ashes in an approaching wave. I read ten books and write every day, sip mezcal, and eat fresh seafood at beachside restaurants with my feet in the sand. I attempt to take Spanish classes, but my foggy brain doesn't cooperate. Every day, I sit by the ocean's edge, marveling at how each day's sunset seems more beautiful than the day before. A gecko appears a few times on my outdoor porch. *Is that you, Suzanne?* I wonder, *with your sticky toe pads, climbing the wall. Did you make it here with me after all?*

I am still in shock and haven't yet felt the heaviness of grief. I haven't even cried much at all. Shock is saving me from collapsing in on myself. It is the great protector. What a marvel is the human body! And it is hard to be sad at the beach.

CHAPTER 24

The Need to Simplify

Northeastern winter, with bone-chilling damp cold and icy mixed precipitation, makes for a challenging re-entry. The brilliant colors of Mexico have disappeared and I am faced with the bleak browns and grays of Philadelphia. I miss the warmth of the sun and I wonder why I have come home to this dismal place.

Plowing forward, I attempt to keep the same schedule I had before Suzanne died—working all my freelance jobs: lomi lomi (Hawaiian massage); face painting for a theater arts company in NYC; teaching English at Berlitz Language School; facilitating dance programs for kids and families in libraries in NY, PA, and NJ; and life modeling at various art schools here in Philly. Just writing the list exhausts me.

At the same time, I begin to work with Pleasance, a holistic health coach, who I had met at a yoga workshop. She suggests that I write a book about grief. Certainly, I know some things—I've lived with Lisa's loss for 17 years and I am muddling my way through the aftermath of Suzanne's suicide. Surely there will be someone who benefits from my sharing.

But first I need to clean up and clear out some things. My floor is carpeted with the paperwork for Suzanne's finances, so I need to work on that. To organize my writing life, I buy a new writing table, which I put together myself. I create a special place in my tiny studio apartment dedicated to writing the book.

I appear to be taking forward steps but gravity works against me. There are days when the exhaustion of grief prevents me from moving. Even lifting my legs to walk seems to take extra effort. Grief's heaviness wears on me, making everything more difficult. My physically challenging massage work seems almost impossible. When I give a session, my heart races from the exertion and my body ends up in Afib.

I realize that I will have to simplify my life. After 19 years of practicing lomi lomi, I let it go and feel relieved. I also become weary of the commute to NYC for the 15-hour face painting days, sometimes for not very much money at all.

And I begin falling down.

The first fall occurs after face painting at Central Park Zoo on a particularly busy summer day where I had little time for breaks and food. The determination to get home quickly, had turned me into one of those running commuters whom I used to mock when I lived there. With no warning, I'm on the ground, the fall partially broken by my suitcase of supplies, always trailing behind me. Luckily I have just a couple of bruises and scrapes. To make it worse, my New Jersey Transit train is cancelled, causing the next train to be overcrowded. I don't get a seat on that train and have to stand all the way from NY to Trenton, where I change trains.

Another fall happens right at home on my way to the garbage room. Carrying more bags than I should have, I'm preoccupied with thoughts other than garbage. Down I go on the carpeted steps, losing hold of the bags. Their contents—mostly paper recyclables—slowly float down around me. It's a sign I am doing too much.

Deep rest is what Pleasance recommends, but I am not getting it. Some things have to change. I have committed to face painting through June, and decide to take the rest of the summer off. When I re-assess the situation In the fall, I don't go back at all.

With a less demanding work life, writing becomes a priority. My foggy grief brain might forget my wallet or my keys, but never my writing book.

First thing in the morning, I write my "morning pages," a habit started in the 90's after my divorce when Julia Cameron's book *The Artist's Way* found its way into my hands. I let my pen chronicle the unedited stream of consciousness—first thoughts, dreams, whatever is there. Clearing out the cobwebs, so I can start the day a little less encumbered.

Later, I make my way to coffee shops with my composition notebooks and Natalie Goldberg's writings. Inspired by her topics and suggestions, I get to process my true feelings. Memories come up and I write. Sometimes, the memory is poignant and tears mix with the ink.

People around me have no idea that I jot down their conversations and describe their quirks or unique traits. Nothing is prohibited in the writing book. Natalie Goldberg's writing method requires you to keep the hand moving, without stopping or editing—to "study" the mind. My grief mind needs a lot of studying! So begins this daily coffee and writing ritual. I get up extra early on work days to make it to the cafe. I am committed. Writing gives me a purpose and I'm inspired to keep going.

CHAPTER 25

Fascination With Suicide

In April of 2018, just eight months after Suzanne's passing, I begin to write a book about my grief. This all-consuming project distracts me from the heaviness that is beginning to crash down around me, as shock starts to dissipate. Because my brain is foggy from grief, I must work slowly and diligently.

The book becomes the place where I can find some structure. Because there is no order, sense, or accuracy in my life, everything is messy. The book motivates me to keep going. I want it to be easy to read and accessible for someone in early grief, whose brain has the same level of fog I have.

First, I make a list of everything I know about grief. This turns into a list of topics, which then becomes the outline for the book. I go back into my composition books, tear out pages, and put them into brightly colored folders arranged by topics.

My brain enjoys the neat little categories and subdivisions from which I tell the stories of grieving Lisa and my real-time impressions of the first year grieving Suzanne. The book is dedicated to my girls, *my greatest teachers.*

It is September, 2018, right after Suzanne's first anniversary, when I finish the draft and begin the editing and self-publishing process. These tasks also require diligence and super focus. Because I am exhausted from grief and technically challenged, I hire a group of talented helpers: editor, cover designer, and formatter, who turn out to be my publishing support group.

Although the book has 275 pages and 11 chapters, not one of them addresses the topic of suicide. Because I wrote this book in early grief, shock prevented me from feeling the enormity and totality of suicide loss.

While engrossed in the book project, anxiety begins to set in, as I am filled with conflicting emotions: love, fear, compassion, anger, sadness, guilt, relief, shame, regret, and remorse. They drip into my body in small doses. The dagger remains in my gut. There are sleepless nights and there is comfort eating. The topic of suicide is overwhelming, so I don't write much about it. I just can't deal with it.

I do want to to learn more about suicide. Whatever happens to me, I read about it. I know that I am never the first one to have experienced something. But, in this state of shock and overwhelm, I feel as if I've been hit by a tsunami. So It's really hard. Maybe I can figure out why Suzanne died this way.

I read tons of books and go to support meetings for survivors of suicide. Everyone tells me that it's not my fault.

My logic tells me that too, but I don't feel it in my bones. I say those words to myself, and even write those words, hoping that I will grow into them. *It is not my fault. It is not my fault.*

Trouble is, Suzanne has told me directly in her journal, in her own handwriting, that it is my fault. I read her words again, "I hate you Mom." I can't handle her anger, so I close the journal again, for now.

And if there is something called *Suicide Prevention,* then I should have been able to prevent it. I teeter on the edge of learning more about prevention, to help others, but feel sick to my stomach, when I think that I will learn all the things I should and could have done. After all, I am the Mother. More prickly and unsettled feelings begin to bubble up and emerge as space begins to open.

As my book project is almost complete, my brain moves to new thoughts. I wonder about other people who died by suicide. *What were they thinking before they died? How is it that they hid their feelings from others? Could someone have prevented their* deaths?

I think about Julie, who I met in New York City in late 2000 at a Compassionate Friends support group a few months after Lisa died. She had lost her only child, a son. There wasn't anything particularly noteworthy or different about Julie, a middle-aged woman like myself. We were all a mess, having lost children of various ages and in various ways, none of them good. I got to know her a little. Later I learned that she arranged to have a retrospective of her artwork in a gallery and invited everyone she knew. It was a wonderful event and well attended. And the next day she jumped off the roof of a high-rise building.

How did she get to a place where she believed that she didn't have one more painting in her? Maybe she was finished. Maybe her brain told her so and she couldn't see past it. I can't get Julie off my mind.

Also, I become obsessed with the book, *What Made Maddy Run,* by Kate Fagan. As I am trying to make sense of Suzanne's suicide, I find some similarities in Maddy's story.

A UPenn athlete, she died by jumping from an upper level of a parking garage in Philadelphia, not far from my apartment. The book pieces together the last moments of Maddy's life. What intrigues me most is that right before she jumped, she visited the college bookstore to buy gifts for her family and friends. She carried them in a brown paper bag to the parking garage and on the way, she met her coach and has a perfectly "normal" conversation with him—he didn't suspect that anything was irregular. Then she went to the garage, left the bag and a note, and jumped.

I think about this young woman because she was so "successful" on the outside and knew how to fool everyone, including the person who saw her minutes before she died. It was the same with Suzanne. Functional until the end. We just don't know what is going on underneath someone's exterior "face." We all have it—that face we put on when we go out into the world, so people won't know about our fear, sadness, guilt, or anything else that we want to hide. We want to appear okay. We must appear okay. We smile and put on a happy face.

I read this book four or five, maybe six times. Partly because grief brain fog prevents me from comprehending all the details. Also, I think that the next time I read it, I will find the answers to make myself feel better. I don't.

The books I read don't provide the answers I seek. David Kessler, grief expert, says that,"… we will never find a satisfactory explanation for suicide." I guess it's similar to saying we will never find a satisfactory explanation for why someone gets cancer or gets hit by a car.

Where does the brain go on such a journey? Very few people have survived jumping off the Golden Gate Bridge, but I read about one survivor's experience. As soon as he jumped, he said, "Oh shit."

Did Maddy have an "Oh shit" moment? Did the artist in NYC?

Did Suzanne have one when she connected herself to the IV with the concoction of drugs that killed her? I don't think there was time for that because her death was instant.

In addition to trying to figure out Suzanne's suicide, I often return to thoughts of these two women, Maddy and

Julie, fascinated by the weird workings of the brain that cause an outwardly "successful" person to make these decisions. I don't realize at this time that I will get so low as to consider suicide myself.

CHAPTER 26

Somewhere in the Void

Autumn, 2018

I *won't jump off the building after I finish my book,
because there is the next book or the next poem or the
next piece of writing that I do.* I write these words in a
notebook. Am I reassuring myself?

I think how easy it is to hide what's inside from others.
And how we will never know the thought process that takes
a person from art show to death; from shopping for gifts to
death; from one day being your daughter, a functioning
nurse anesthetist, to death. Even people with *lived
experience* of suicide (those who survived attempts) say that
they don't know themselves, how they got to that point.

As my time is not so focused now, I notice myself writing
more about suicide in my journals. I begin to mention the
Empty Space, the Void, the desert in front of me and the
only way to navigate it is one day at a time, sometimes one
hour at a time, because my book project has delayed the big
feelings.

Also, I start to realize that I am now childless. Losing Lisa
was hard, really hard, but I still had Suzanne. It's a concept

that is difficult to grasp. Who am I without any children? Do I even exist?

On the top shelf of my closet is a stack of travel journals that I had specifically written thinking that one day Suzanne would find them. Now, when I die, who will read them? Will they end up in the trash? As parents we do so many things with our kids' futures in mind. When their futures are no more, what becomes of us?

On the first cold day in October the sudden temperature drop feels harsh. I notice that everything is getting harder. It feels like the world is coming to an end, and maybe it is or maybe I am.

The only problem with writing a book is it ends, but my life experiences keep going. The world keeps going. Record numbers of people show up for early voting. Some Republicans turn Democrat and Trump still pays people to go to his rallies. All of this can be going on while I mourn the loss of my daughter and search for the crunchiest apple at the farmers' market.

Last year at this time, I had my floor covered with papers, working on Suzanne's finances. That's finished. I had a wonderful relationship with a lawyer in Denver, and with Pleasance, who helped me begin the book. Those relationships are pretty much over. Now, it's just me. Maybe I need more help, but I don't know what that will be.

In The Void, I wonder if I am finished, the way Julie was. I've written the book, contacted all the people who helped me after Lisa died and all the people who help me now, and maybe I am just done. Will I feel like jumping off a building? Luckily I don't live in a high-rise and I'm not likely to walk on a bridge and jump.

I can't think of any acceptable way that I would kill myself so I guess I don't want to die. I also don't want to feel bad, so I have to start reaching out—find a boyfriend, something, just for a distraction.

What is this fascination with suicide by jumping? I have always been fearful of getting to the edge of a high place like at the Empire State Building or at Niagara Falls. A weird feeling, like if I get too close, I might just jump—just to see. I'm not sure what that is. Or why I seem to have a fascination for the jumping suicides and not the pill taking ones or the gunshot ones. Some people might say that I had an experience in a past life, which has given me memories. Who knows? Focusing on these other suicides keeps me from thinking about Suzanne's.

On a chilly November evening, I walk out into the Friday vibe of the city and suddenly feel lonely. Everyone is having their weekend and I have nowhere to go and no one to be with. A profound sadness comes over me and it suddenly becomes clear how you could get so low that you kill yourself in a moment of despair.

***

It's my last model job for the semester and my body has been resisting the energy required to get myself up in the early morning and out into the chilling air. The season has been screaming at me to Stop/ Slow Down/ Rest.

Deep in thought, I lose my balance on the way to the bus stop. A homeless man, who takes his post every morning at the traffic light, notices me. I teeter and sway and somehow catch myself before what could have been a crushing descent to the concrete pavement. All those years of ballet and yoga have paid off in this moment.

The homeless man looks up from the cars that he has been stopping to ask for money. He seems mesmerized by my athletic and dancer-like display

"Whoa" he says.

"Whoa" I echo.

Rest is coming.

I am putting the finishing touches on the book. In my head I am writing acknowledgements and words for the back cover. So my head and feet are in totally different places. And the good thing about the almost fall is that it wakes me up to my aliveness, brings me out of my funk. Fear gives me energy. Weird. Whoa!

I make a mental note to be more mindful. After a crowded bus ride, squashed up against people standing in the front, I am relieved to have an easy modeling session, a clothed portrait pose.

I take my seated position on the model stand and begin to fall into a deep meditative relaxation. Modeling can be a very restful job. Meanwhile, the teacher lectures. I go in and out of paying attention to her words. At one point, she references an exhibition that she had seen at the Frick Collection in NYC. She describes one painting there as "about 1 1/2 times the size of Roberta." There is an extended period of silence in the room, as the students continue to draw.

Then, a deep voice sounds from behind an easel in the back."So, Roberta has become a unit of measurement?"

I start to crack up, finding the sensibility of this joke the most hysterical thing that I have heard in a long time, perhaps in my whole life. I am trying to be professional, but my whole body gives into deep belly laughing. Had that continued, I would have gone into tears rolling down my face, maybe a deep cry. A release is a release. And laughing and crying have always been connected for me. By now, the whole room is laughing. And I am noticing how very strange and foreign it is to laugh, and yet, also very natural. And how much I need this.

I am able to compose myself and go on with the pose, but the laughter had done the trick.... for the moment. Thank you anonymous art student at UPenn.

I chuckle the rest of the day and even now years later, it brings a smile to my face.

CHAPTER 27

Grouchy

In December I complete and upload my book to Amazon and now want to treat myself to a celebratory coffee at my favorite cafe. It is a busy Saturday, due to the weekly farmers' market across the street. Typically, I avoid this place on the weekends, but decide to take a chance.

I watch and wait patiently for a table to open up, and when someone gets up, I begin to move toward the available space, but someone else does the same.

"Are you alone?" the neatly dressed man asks me in an irritated voice.

"I've been waiting for the table," I offer. I surmise that this man and his friend, who were already seated, preferred this particular table.

"Are you alone?" he asks again with a little extra impatience. Once is enough. Dangerous question for a mother who has lost both her children. I could have said many things:

Rude- "It's none of your business."

Spiritual- "I'm never alone."

Logical- "What difference does it make?"

I think of all of those options afterwards, as I usually do. The thoughtless question takes me by surprise. Doesn't a single person have the same table rights as two people? I didn't expect that those words would just sit on my heart the way they did, reminding me, I was very much alone.

I had been silenced.

I respond to the clueless individual with one word. "Yes," and then head to the exit as fast as I can. At the last second, I face him and blurt out, in my best competitive, snarky tone, "Why don't you just take the table?" Then turn my back with a dramatic flourish, leave, and vow never again to go back there on a Saturday.

In retrospect, I should have left when I saw how crowded the place was. And noisy. Headache inducing noisy. I don't have the energy for that. Even the crowds at the Farmers' Market are stressful and exhausting.

I am already lonely and angry and this man has thrown it in my face. In fairness, he has no idea what I am going through. Getting a table in a city coffee shop can be a cutthroat experience, and clearly at this moment, I can't handle it.

I am well aware that the holidays loom. And all the expectations that come with the season, and all of what's missing is front and center. It is why I like to travel this time of year—something to look forward to that's not about holidays. Planning and preparing for a trip around this time is always a good idea. And I can't get back to Mexico fast enough.

✱✱✱

When I return to Playa Zicatela for the second year in a row, grouchiness comes with me. Last year, the place was salvation because shock protected me. With shock wearing off and reality setting in, I am raw. There is a galaxy of Empty Space here at the beach, away from my desk, computer, TV, and work. Now I am prickly and unsettled and noticing everything I overlooked in the fog of early grief last year. I have become a bouncy house for fear and sadness, guilt and grouchiness.

Initially, I am blissfully positive. *Last year was about recovery,* I write, *this year is about discovery,* but I notice that almost everything I *discover* bothers me. If I am honest, the trip is part nightmare and part adventure.

My accommodations this year are different. For 40 bucks a night, I can't complain. This bungalow has an outdoor covered kitchen and a porch with table facing a tropical garden and the beach below. There's a fridge, a gas hot plate on a table, and a huge jug of purified water on the counter. The shower offers a gentle trickle of warmish water.

My bathroom is connected by a door to my bedroom, but has an additional "door," a blanket, facing the outdoor kitchen. *Is it not enough that my heart is exposed?*

On my first night, an obstructed view of the sunset at my favorite beach restaurant puts me in a sour mood. And the crowds! Why are there so many people here?

I want to scream or run when the beach bar next to the restaurant plays music with a buzzing heavy bass that vibrates my table. And I am just trying to eat my fish tacos! How rude!! The thumping sound goes right through my body and assaults every cell.

At midday, the sun, is too bright, causing the sand to hurt my feet. The nerve of that sun!

And who's to say that the little cockroach hiding behind my hand towel every night, doesn't deserve to have that as his resting place? But every night I am shocked and repulsed.

In my four weeks at the beach, I have one panic attack and two Afib episodes each lasting about six hours, and have no TV to distract me from the discomfort.

The nights are the hardest.

Sleep is fitful and with no distractions from my thoughts. I go over everything I should have, could have, and would have done differently over the years of being with my daughter, especially at the end. Tears cascade down my face like an avalanche on Everest. My body shakes with the profound depth of sadness, a sadness I had avoided while writing my book. I had cried, but not like this.

To top things off, a few days into the trip, Montezuma has his way with me and gifts me with a severe bout of his "revenge," causing my stomach to be "off" for a good half of the trip. So I cry about that, too. I am one big exploding mess of fluids. *Why did I leave my cozy little apartment for this hell?*

Music on my phone and yoga nidra sessions on YouTube help me sleep some nights. If I am lucky, I'll get a couple of hours.

I arrive in late December, so this will be a most unglamorous New Year's Eve, not that I make a big deal of the last day of the year. I miss all the festivities in town. No worries. I watch the pink sunset of the last day of 2018 from my porch while eating cucumbers and sardines, maybe not the best choice for my restless stomach. And the music from the beach bars and restaurant parties is loud enough to reach my bungalow on the top of the hill. The party goes on all night. My New Year's is tears instead of bubbly and trips to the toilet instead of dancing. I can only hope for a little shut eye.

The giant fan, powered with hurricane force, thankfully keeps away the mosquitos and also drowns out the music. If I leave it on, I freeze. Turn it off and I get covered in bites. Which sounds better?

On New Year's Day, an email jumps out at me—there's an unexpected notification on my credit report that someone has opened a new account in my name.That freaks me out. *Who would do that? How will I be able to handle this from Mexico?* I am already a mess. Every experience is heightened and I immediately become afraid.

With no success getting through to the listed phone numbers, a kind Verizon representative helps me navigate the problem. It turns out that 800 numbers don't work when you're in Mexico. She makes the call and connects me to the credit card company. I find out they had upgraded my original account without my permission, which shows up as a new account. So, after five hours on the phone trying a million different numbers and chatting with the Verizon operator, no mystery person has stolen my identity.

I am the mystery person. That's about right!

Welcome, 2018!

CHAPTER 28

Not All Bad

Looking for some comfort, I get on the phone with my friends from home. Also I hear from a Philly yoga studio that wants to host the "grief" workshop I have created. This is a big deal, because I believe that sharing my story and guiding others will help me find a new purpose in life and make some sense of my loss. It's a fine idea, but I don't realize how silly it is that this blubbering person will be the one in charge of the group. *Fake it till you make it,* in full action. That was part of the plan. Finish the book, do the grief workshops, and everything will be fine. A nice little package. But I am so far from fine.

In my sleepless nights I research Afib. I learn that it can be triggered by big emotional fight or flight responses, even a day later. That makes sense. I also discover that acupuncture is a tool that helps Afib and make a mental note to arrange a few sessions when I get home. My research tells me the best prevention for Afib is happiness!! Easier said than done.

When I get home, I will tell everyone how bad this trip was, but my writing says otherwise. Memory can play tricks.

The nights are hellish, but the morning light washes away the negativity. The dawn's yellow/orange glow spreads over the tropical garden that I can see from the window over my bed. I marvel at its beauty. I sip green tea on the porch and watch a hummingbird fly from flower to flower in search of the best nectar. Ancient faces emerge from the trunks of trees and giant coconuts, rich and ripe, sit atop the palms. Yellow butterflies flutter about. I can hear the ocean from my bed.

The horrible nights morph into more pleasant days when I venture down to the beach in early mornings and late afternoons. It is as if I am living in two separate universes.

A long flight of stone stairs descends to a small passageway which leads to the beach. A few birds drink from the small trickle of water that runs down the middle of the walkway. Pink bougainvillea lines the path. It is a pleasant and shady walk. Last year I was greeted by sleeping dogs on the path. This year, birds and butterflies have claimed it.

Early mornings, before the sun gets too hot, the beach is empty. I write. I count pelicans. Sometimes there are three or five flying. One time there were 11, making their swooping hungry flights for fish dinner, dipping down into the waves which are sometimes very high.

On one of my daily sunset beach walks, I encounter a lone pelican, an aging fellow, near the rocks. As he looks more like a Disney character than a real bird, I'm not sure if he is injured or just old. He seems content to let people go about their business while his wrinkled self stands silent and motionless in the sand. *Abuelo Pelican,* I call him. *Grandfather. Are you waiting for something?* Every time I take a step towards him, he moves a step back. *Keep your distance,* Abuelo is warning me. Why is he so far from his flock?

There are always surfers waiting for the perfect wave. In summer Playa Zicatela is a coveted hot spot when the waves are at their highest, but in winter it is quieter.

One morning I notice a man on a paddle board. Now, we're talking the strong waves of the Pacific Ocean here. He isn't a young man, from what I can see, but he is familiar with the waves. He has done this before. Balancing himself as the waves shift and flow requires constant vigilance. One tiny distraction would have him lose footing and topple over. That is a rare occurrence. I am in awe of his commitment. I imagine he must reap such joy from his skill. Pelicans swoop down near him and he remains steady on the board.

At the water's edge, a brown fisherman has some luck. Every time he pulls in his net, there are at least two flopping shiny silver fish measuring 12 inches or more, and he puts them in the bag on his waist.

As another man runs out into the waves. I worry. *What will he do when the big one comes?* He dives under them. What a technique. No fear. A few dives, a few big waves, and now he's out.

Although I'm an excellent swimmer in the still water of a pool or lake, I have no idea how to swim in the ocean. I say I have respect for it, but it's fear. I still remember when I was five and got sucked out and down into the ocean at the Jersey Shore. My father just couldn't hold onto my hand when the powerful wave came. The Atlantic Ocean churned me around and the undertow pulled me out a bit. Before my petrified father could rescue me, I got an unappetizing mouthful of sand and salt, which I never forgot. I don't know that we ever told my mother.

After that, my parents made sure I learned how to swim, but never in the ocean. Now I just wander out a little bit to get wet if it's hot, then hurry back to my blanket.

One morning I don't see Paddleboard Man, but I do see a solitary swimmer way out. It appears that this person has some flotation/safety device close by in case of exhaustion, probably. This swimmer makes constant horizontal movements across the Pacific. What stamina and dedication! Again I am in awe.

I ponder Paddleboard Man's experience compared to the surfers'. Surfers have a lot a patience. They study the waves and take a chance when the moment is right. They balance for a brief moment of thrill, that brings them back again and again.

Paddleboard Man's experience involves no waiting. He works continuously for homeostasis, to find his footing on the constantly moving ocean. It's not the thrill for him — it's just the being, the maintaining. He floats on top of the ocean as he finds his balance. Afterward, maybe he thinks, "Wow, I have just floated on the ocean," or maybe, "Wow my calves or shoulders sure do hurt right now." And then he shows up the next day for more.

I wonder if my life is more like Paddleboard Man's or Surfer's, and think definitely Paddleboard Man's. I teeter on the edge of my emotions finding calm some of the time, and crashing down other times. It is a constant balancing act to find some grace while the waves keep coming.

A dragonfly greets me at the beach. Dragonfly is my sign from Lisa. Where is Suzanne here?

CHAPTER 29

The Company of Dogs

I'm attempting to boil a chicken breast and white rice on the outdoor kitchen's hotplate, for my "Zuma" diet, but the breeze keeps putting out the fire. I light it over and over. The breeze is welcomed on this hot day, but it is also frustrating and makes me grouchy that I have to stand guard over my meal. I use so many matches, I have to purchase a new box.

While wishing I was glamping, not camping, Malo, the resident dog (named "Bad" because of his mischievous behavior), finds his way to my porch. A medium-sized mixed breed with short brown fur, he sits and waits, assuming that he is entitled to a portion of what I'm cooking. Unable to resist those big brown eyes, I give him the boiled chicken skin and he gobbles it up. He wanders in and out to check on who is entering the school, but when he smells my cooking, he always returns, eternally hopeful that he will receive more. Once I put the cooling chicken breast in the fridge, he finally goes. Smart dog. And optimistic. Keeps hoping maybe there are a few more morsels for his mouth.

He doesn't only visit me at meal times. In fact, the hanging blanket between my bathroom and kitchen, provides easy access for Malo, when he wants to check on me. He comes right into my bedroom for a pet or ear rub. Of course, I enjoy his attention.

As bad as my stomach feels, and as grouchy as I am about the wind taking out the flames while I'm cooking, I am grateful for the company of dogs.

Malo, who becomes my bestie, graduates from boiled skin to a few chicken pieces that "unexpectedly" "fall" to the floor. Eventually he gets his own bowl with chicken and rice and some broth. He's now a daily companion. He sleeps at my feet while I eat, never begging.

One morning when he wanders in at breakfast, I have nothing for him. Then I remember the dog biscuit in my winter coat pocket leftover from a visit with a friend's dog. Malo has to have it. When I tell him to sit and wait for his treat, it seems as if he understands every word. He waits patiently until I return with his biscuit and he crunches it quickly, then leaves. We are building a relationship.

Two weeks in, I dream about me feeding him chicken and rice.

At Coste, a restaurant on the beach, two other dogs wander in to keep me company—one sleeps at my feet under the table and the other one rests behind me. They are not begging for food. Maybe they live at this restaurant. Everyone lets their dogs wander freely so it's hard to tell. I feel so comforted by their presence.

Did Suzanne send them to me?

I think it is only fitting that Suzanne should come to me here in dog form. In addition to loving her own dogs, my granddogs Dutchie and Mully, she helped other dogs get rescued. On one of my Dallas visits, we helped out a rescue organization by checking in on some shelter dogs. As we walked around, looking at all the caged canines, Suzanne chose the ones that looked the most lonely and forlorn. She entered their kennels to give them some love and pets. We took them out, and walked them around, taking photos for the organization's website. "One day," she mused, "I would like to have my own rescue."

One morning a little brown beach dog comes to visit me as I lay on my sarong at the water's edge. *Suzanne, are you behind this?* I feed him some water from my hand. Eventually, he licks my hand and lets me pet him. He lays down right next to me, decides to dig a little to get to cooler wetter sand, and then puts his body in the hole. The sand sprays onto my sarong as he digs, but I don't let it bother me because the moment is so precious. When he is finished, the pile of sand becomes his pillow and he rests there, next to me.

Suddenly, his body becomes alert—he hears something—a police vehicle driving down the beach. He is now my protector, jumping up and running towards the vehicle, barking until it goes away. Then he comes back, digs a fresh hole and settles himself back in.

When another police vehicle comes by in a few minutes, my little friend tries to race with it. He loses, of course. He has ended up far away but finds his way back. This time as he digs his new hole, he gets sand on my thigh. The little sand pile is now as close to me as it can be and he rests his head there. *Little sweetness. Do you want to come home with me?*

After a while he gets up and unceremoniously walks away—no goodbye, no nothing. I watch him for a little while as he finds some shade under a lounge chair closer to the restaurant behind us. The chair is inhabited by a shirtless man with a protruding belly, so he gets full shade there, but this man wants no part of the dog. He kicks sand at him and eventually, my dog buddy leaves for the shade of a table at a restaurant.

When I feel better and begin to venture out for meals, Malo shows up to my kitchen and looks sad that there is no food cooking. I wonder if he will miss me, but I think I will miss him more. He will mostly miss the boiled chicken.

CHAPTER 30

My Revolution

B y the last week of my trip, my energy is back and I am
feeling more myself. The idea of canceling some of my
Spanish classes to have more beach time seems like a divine
choice. Feeling "normal" makes me bold. I am exhilarated,
re-charged, and renewed.

It's the Revolution of Roberta. I am breaking out and
breaking free and the beach is where it happens.

In Spanish class, I have bonded with my teacher whom
I have seen every day for three hours. We talk about
everything, but in Spanish—her English is not good—and I
want her to understand my frustration. Trying to explain
"grouchy" to her is futile as there is no exact translation—
there's *hypersensitive, irritable*, and *angry*. It's kind of all
three of those. She has never heard of Oscar the Grouch, so
that doesn't help.

So I cut down the number of class hours and send the
teacher home—with full pay, of course. With my renewed
vitality, I run to the beach in the late afternoons just to get
wet in the surf.

Turns out that Revolution pours out of my molecules and spills out into the air, creating an energy that says to the world *I am sexy.* While devouring a delicious *hamburguesa*, the restaurant's owner, a much younger man, introduces himself. He walks me out when I am ready to go and kisses me on the cheek.

"Have you been to Puerto Manzanilla? Puerto Angelito?

"No."

"Would you like to?"

"No, gracias—" I cut him right off, because I am having my own personal Revolution and I make the decisions.

I wake up early the next morning, just before sunlight enters my window, with a dream that I am in the arms of a younger lover. Nice!

Finding normal again, after a questionable, unpredictable stomach, feels like a superpower. I walk around with a smile on my face. *This is what the vacation was supposed to feel like.*

How about a massage? Yes. This is exactly what my healing body needs! I wander around this tiny beach town and notice a sign for massages. So, I make my way to Tacho, the Oaxacan native massage guy. Turns out he treats my Spanish teacher, so it's all in the family. I make an appointment.

This surge of energy, the new power of my Revolution, creates a false sense of security on the beach. Even though there is no lifeguard, I go out a little further than usual. A wave knocks me down and then tries to pull me out because of course it does. My inexperience in ocean swimming shows. There is a moment of intense fear when I feel like I will be swept out to sea and no one will find me. With my left foot firmly dug deep into the sand, I fight with the Pacific Ocean. Ha! This produces nothing but pain. The current twists my leg, affecting the muscle around my knee. I will have to reveal this information to Tacho before the massage so he knows just how to work on me.

In the fragrant backyard garden at Tacho's modest dwelling, I rest on the massage table under a pergola, a wooden structure with a fabric-covered roof. The distant sounds of children playing, birds singing, dogs barking, and the ocean roaring provide the soundtrack. With a generous helping of oil and strong experienced hands, I am transported. Every part of my body gets massaged: breasts, lower belly, and of course my twisted knee. Tacho constantly checks in to see if I am okay. I am so much better than okay. Honoring every part of me. Letting myself be open and serenaded by the sea.

I decide to go back for one more massage session the next day. *Why not?* I leave for home the day after. Two massages solidify the Revolution.

On my last evening at the beach, I go to my favorite restaurant for some fish tacos and choose a wicker couch with a low table, where I can put my toes in the sand. While I am enjoying a glass of mezcal, served with peanuts and orange slices, I have a sense that I am not alone. I look underneath the couch and see my little amigo dog from the beach. Whether he found me or I found him, I take it as a gift from Suzanne that we have this moment together at my farewell dinner. He stays under my seat the whole time.

During my last night's sleep, an Afib episode wakes me up. I try to figure out the trigger. *Too much of a good thing? The intense fear as I battled the ocean? Stress about having to return to my regular life?*

Sometimes there is no answer.

CHAPTER 31

Beyond Grouchy

R e-entry from Mexico is difficult. A bleak and dismal winter greets me with its cold grayness, and I must return to work. No more sun, clear blue skies, spectacular sunsets, and sipping mezcal on the beach. No more visits from friendly dogs *Didn't I just have a Revolution?* The memory of it fades quickly. The spark of life that came into me at the beach begins to fizzle out. *Did I dream it?*

Grouchiness returns and takes over. What I remember most about Mexico are the annoyances, the "revenge," and the deep wells of grief which finally spill out of me.

At least I still have my morning ritual—sipping coffee while reading and writing in my favorite coffee shops around the city.

Good Karma, with its peaceful vibe, is one of my favorite spots. It sits on the Walnut Street Bridge, a short walk from my apartment. At a window seat, I can watch the people and cars pass by. A statue of a smiling Buddha rests on a bathroom cabinet. In the main area, college students study silently.

On this particular day just after returning home from Mexico, I find myself out of sorts and without any patience. In fact, I am really pissed at the man sitting two seats away from me—basically because he exists.

I feel like I'm part of his long loud phone conversation, which distracts me while I try to read and write. I give him a disapproving "look" now and then. He lowers his voice for a minute but the volume steadily increases. *No, the entire coffee shop does not want to hear your conversation, Sir!*

Plus, he slurps his coffee.

And sniffles—*get a tissue, will ya.*

And sighs, way too loudly.

He has become my enemy and everything his human body does threatens me, but he doesn't know it.

I could move my seat—mostly everyone has left—but no. I'll let myself stay here and be annoyed.

I am just grouchy. Maybe I will be grouchy forever. Is this the new me? I am grouchy because my daughter died and I couldn't do anything to stop it. I am grouchy because I am getting old and feel like I am disappearing. And now, I'm grouchy because I've finished the book, and that didn't make me less grouchy. In fact, maybe I'm even more grouchy because I don't have it as a distraction.

To add to the list, our president is destroying our country. And I've made a couple of typos in my book and I can't do anything about that either. And now, I am even more grouchy And my enemy is back on the phone and sniffling again.

Loudly.

Just to annoy me.

* * *

Feb, 2019

"I was thinking, why do we even *need* the model stand?" the teacher says to me when I report for my job on the UPenn campus on a freezing February day. They have changed the room for the class, but haven't moved the model stand.

"If you are standing over time on a hard floor, it's not good for your body." I explain it to her, even though I know she knows it. I am getting ready to disrobe and pose for the class.

I have modeled for this teacher before and I like her, but this is only the second time she is teaching the drawing class and I can see clearly that she doesn't have a clue how to teach it. Her specialty is painting. Having been a classroom teacher for 15 years, and even trained a student teacher, I have some experience. And since 2009 when I began modeling as a part-time job, I have been in hundreds of drawing classes and seen the good, the bad, and the ugly. This one was ugly. And I am grouchy.

"How's your book selling?" she inquires.

I hate her. She is the biggest enemy of my day. "Where is your tan from Mexico?" Now she gives me the double whammy, reminding me that I am not a marketing whiz and my tan has faded. *She must really hate me.* I can feel my body temperature increase as my face reddens.

When I posed for her painting class recently, she had been so very interested in my book. "Let me know when it's published. Be sure to let me know when it's published. Don't forget to let me know." It was a really big build-up for me, but when I did let her know, she didn't buy the book. And now she wants to know how it's selling.

I am so past grouchy. Now, I am fuming.

I hate her. And I hate that I have agreed to model for this early morning class in a tiny crowded room with a bad teacher who is too distracted and selfish to think about what the model needs.

When I get home I feel burned out. *Do I have chronic fatigue or fibromyalgia?* I feel unbalanced and out of whack. And it is not just my heart. Every nerve cell feels wrong.

When will this end?

CHAPTER 32

Coming up Cubist

C ubism, according to Merriam Webster, is *a style of art that stresses abstract structure at the expense of other pictorial elements especially by displaying several aspects of the same object simultaneously and by fragmenting the form of depicted objects.*

While modeling at Drexel's art school in an easy pose, a clothed head study, the students are busy taking measurements with skewers. I had high hopes for these students, but many unintentionally draw me as rigid head planes with sharp angular lines that change direction with no connection to reality. They give me oversized eyes, a protruding nose, Martian ears, and exaggerated wrinkles.

Their novice skills reveal some truth. I am as twisted and confused inside as their drawings depict. In one instant, I am vulnerable, at the edge of a sobbing outburst. In another moment I can laugh. In another I am seething with anger. I am both terrified and excited about what is coming next.

Maybe Cubist is what I am—abstract and fragmented. On any given day I feel crushed and jubilant, defeated and energized, hopeful and despondent. I see a visual representation of this in the drawings. The terror of a childless life mixes with passion, a need to have my experiences help others. And I wonder If I have that right to help others or if I am ready. *If I feel responsible for Suzanne's death, does that make me a fraud?* I am in this place of wanting things to happen faster than they are happening.

I don't realize how much I need to heal.

A few students manage to find some softness in their drawings with gentle shading of the dark and erasing to bring in the light. There is vulnerability there. From darkness comes light, sculpting form, sometimes soft, sometimes sharp and harsh.

In my book, I listed about 20 activities that "help" with grief. I have acquired a huge toolbox, since 2000, when Lisa died. Laughter and forgiveness are on the list, and I realize that although I have forgiven Suzanne, I have not forgiven myself. And there just isn't much laughing these days.'

The world has gone grey and lifeless.

I find some relief at the local dog park along the Schuylkill River, a tributary of the Delaware River, just a few blocks from my apartment.

It is usually a joyous place for me — tons of dogs running after balls, playing in the pools, sniffing every other dogs's butt, happy to be free and dogging without restriction. When I remember to go there, my mood lifts.

On this particular day, as I look down from the bridge, the carefree energy of the park shifts with a scuffle between a pit bull and a Doberman. These things happen sometimes when an animal hasn't been properly socialized and usually, they are settled when the owner removes the troublesome dog.

But, today testosterone takes over and the men begin to fight with fists.

I don't see the punch—everything happens so fast and I focus on the action. The pitbull's owner is poised like a boxer, dukes up, one foot in front of the other, knees bent, ready to strike.

Clearly he is the more experienced fighter. What provoked him? Was it just instinct or perhaps self-defense training that kicked in? Or did it have nothing to do with the dogs?

Often, this kind of anger is not about the situation of the moment. I'm aware of that as my anger comes out inappropriately in coffee shops and other places. My daughter died by suicide less than 18 months ago. I can be mad at you, even if you didn't have anything to do with it, because I am mostly angry with myself.

The pit bull owner isn't finished, but while Doberman Daddy is on his phone (prob calling the cops), Pit Bull Daddy begins to leave.

"I'll take you down. I'll fuckin' kill you."

He continues to threaten Doberman Daddy as he makes his way out of the park, taking his time, looking behind him to see if he is being followed. Eventually, Doberman Daddy exits too, in the opposite direction.

I can't stop thinking of the backstories of these guys. Perhaps someone is dealing with a recent death, a divorce, a betrayal, or just simply mental illness or even drug use. Both men were triggered. What happens in their body chemistry that causes the fight, flight, or freeze response? They went right into fight mode. Fast.

Everything in the park goes back to normal after they leave.

I see my anger in the anger of these men and remind myself that I should find the acupuncture that I had read about in Mexico. By keeping anger inside, it gets activated at the littlest provocation—with very unpleasant results, possibly even dangerous ones. And if you don't have someone to physically fight with, how else might this anger express itself?

CHAPTER 33

Invisible

As I move through my day from coffee shop to model job, I start to notice how anger stews inside me with no appropriate place to go.

I'm in a Starbucks on the Drexel campus when two young women get under my skin. Although I don't put up my fists or curse them out, I do speak harshly. Most people who know me consider me pretty even-tempered. When I get angry, I usually speak it and then let it go. But this time, I can't let it go. So, what do I do? I write a story at the cafe. Writing about my feelings usually helps, but the nature of this story is like nothing I have ever written before.

The story, "Invisible Woman"…

When the woman took a seat along at the window of the campus Starbucks, staring at midwinter's bleak grayness, she was already on edge. It hadn't yet been two years since the loss of her daughter to suicide and the feelings were complicated and unprocessed, and getting worse. She positioned herself on a stool between two J. Crew-clad college girls, their heads bent over their computers. She placed her steaming cup of decaf and her writing book in front of her. Writing usually helped to sort things out.

The girls, like twin bookends, simultaneously lifted their heads from their studies and began a conversation around her as if she weren't there. Her old self would have offered to change seats so the girls could talk more easily, but this new strange, uncomfortable identity was infuriated.

"Do you really have to do that? It's rude." The words spat out of her mouth like piercing knives. Did they really not see the graying woman between them? In their minds, she thought, she didn't count—may as well have been just an empty chair. Certainly not a person.

The woman had already begun to feel invisible. She couldn't pinpoint when it began, that feeling. But sometime in the season, when she wasn't busy, little moments of emptiness came up. She felt these unsettling feelings gnaw at her, feelings she couldn't define and didn't want to deal with. It was all too much.

That's when she began to disappear. Or to imagine it.

Was she getting physically smaller? Would there be one day when she got so small that she could hide in a dust mote or on a dew drop on a spider's web and listen to petty conversations of beautiful coeds?

She imagined getting thin, so thin that she could lay flat against the wall and would appear to be the latest design in wall decor.

So thin that she could lie on a coffee shop table where students would rest their lattes and muffins on her. And leave their crumbs and drips.

For the moment she sipped her decaf. One of the college girls rose from her stool and walked around her, to continue their conversation, now in hushed tones. The woman's harsh scolding had forced the girls to acknowledge her. For a moment, she felt the presence of her body sitting on the stool. Her body still had form. After a bit, the young coeds returned to their seats and bowed their heads back into their electronic devices, their overly loud and seemingly important conversation, on pause.

Not from the mind of the woman.

Unable to let go of the feeling, she thought about other times she felt this way— ignored—in her marriage, for one. Perhaps the feelings went deeper than that.

Childless.

She didn't use the word much, but it was true. She had lost her only other child, also a daughter, 17 years before the recent loss. And it was just starting to dawn on her that having no children is much worse and lonelier. Who was she now that both her kids were gone? A woman of a certain age, does not have to sink so deep into the rocking chair so that she becomes it.

"Stupid college kids," she thought. "I'll show them! I will not be invisible to them."

There will be revenge!

This is the Revolution,

The Revolution of me!

She took another sip of her decaf and looked around. Which was the tallest building? Hmmm let's see. Which one could she easily get to the top of? One with a parking garage. Perfect.

She finished her drink and gathered her things. She only had to walk a couple of blocks until she found City Parking on Chestnut and 31st Street and easily took the elevator to the top floor, 14th. That would work.

I am not invisible.

It was a slow, creaky elevator, but finally she walked out. Only a few cars were parked on this level. She had a perfect view of The Drexel and UPenn Campuses and the Schuykilll River running through the city.

She thought about jumping.

She thought about moving to the edge, stepping on the concrete rail, looking up then down, then ever so slowly leaning forward until gravity took over.

She would show those pretty coeds, the ones who weren't all that smart, but had rich daddies who knew people to get them into college. Those who viewed college more as a fashion opportunity, than as an opportunity to learn.

Those girls would be so sad when they heard about the suicide. It would be all over the news, and when they saw the photo (if they watched the news), they would think, oh that was the lady we ignored in Starbucks, who snapped at us when we were trying to have a conversation. They would think, what if we didn't have that rude conversation over her head?

What about her own kids? What would they think? Well, they were already gone, so no need to worry about them.

It was an unseasonably warm, yet gloomy February day. She opened a few buttons on her grey wool coat, which was now too tight for her.

I am not invisible.

She looked down over the city of Philadelphia. It had changed so much over the years. Neighborhoods once gruff and gritty had been taken over by artists, hipsters, and young professionals. From vacant lots rose shiny glass, metal and concrete buildings that filled in along the river, changing the skyline.

She was no longer young. On a dull and damp February day, she could feel the possibility of a disappearing life. There was a boldness in the quest to stop a disappearance. Some kind of justice.

The thoughts seemed logical at the time.

She stood there a long while, it seemed. The impulse for revenge by death started to wane. She realized that it would be a sloppy ending to her life.

But that light in us, she thought, it never really goes out, does it?

Someone dies and we feel them. We remember them— how we laughed with them, cried with them, how they made us feel. Sometimes it wasn't perfect. We got angry and yelled. Then we apologized. What if we don't get the chance to apologize?

For a while, anger gives us something to live for. Something or someone to blame. We yell at them and maybe at God.

Who would yell if this woman jumped? In that moment she couldn't think of anyone. Some friends, a few remaining relatives, but they might find it more sad than anything. They would mostly cry and try to figure out why. They would think they should have and could have done something— made that phone call or sent that last email.

Sometimes a bad mood can dissipate. Sometimes it lingers like a foggy mist on a mountain top. Sometimes you feel small, like you are disappearing, and then two clueless college students ignore your presence, and you feel worse.

With her jacket unbuttoned, the woman felt a bit of warmth on her skin. A few rays of sun had broken through the hovering clouds. Back in her body, she sensed the concrete below her feet and the force of gravity keeping her there.

A hint of spring filled the air with the scent of possibility.

It was not in her nature to end this way. She doesn't know how she will end, but no one does. She took the elevator down to the ground floor, and walked out into the University City streets. It was lunchtime and she was hungry.

PART III

Starting Over

CHAPTER 34

Acupuncture Journey

After scaring myself shitless by writing that story, I don't waste any more time. I don't want to die, but I know I'm thinking too much about suicide. With heightened levels of emotion, illogical solutions can seem normal. Because I want to have a healthy relationship with my daughter on the Other Side, while remaining on *this* side, I need to take care of myself.

In the 90's when I was in a different kind of overwhelm—a divorce and attempting to handle two kids gone wild—a friend told me to try holotropic breathwork, an intense breathing technique that helps to release anger. It changed my life. I had never heard of it and had no clue what it was before I stepped into the room. Around the same time, my friend Lorraine packed me into a car for my first trip to Kriplau. Again, I had no clue what I'd be in for. It was so much more than a "yoga place," as I called it. I said Yes to both because I knew I was in trouble. And I was scared.

This moment is like that. I am in a deep state of overwhelm and have to find my way out. So I say yes to acupuncture.

Stick some needles in.

Less is more.

Let me be still in this dark space,

in this safe place.

Let me be healed.

The name of my first treatment, "Clearing out the Demons," doesn't sound relaxing. You would think the demons might fight back. It is all too complicated for me, so I allow myself to surrender to Dr. B., who has been recommended by a caring friend.

Thoughts come to my mind, but the meditative state of the session lets them pass. My mind empties. I desperately need deep rest.

After the session, my body feels like it is a million years old and weighs 2000 pounds. I am finally crashing down. By 9PM I am asleep and have one of my recurring teaching dreams …

I'm in the main office and I have forgotten to check my mailbox "Where are the keys?" I ask a colleague. She points to a pile of little felt drawstring bags. There are only a few left—one is mine. In the contents of my bag are coins and other small objects including two keys on a shiny ring, but they look too big.

When my eyes open my heart is racing. What does this mean? I am looking forward to the next session.

Dr. B. says that she is including the treatment for depression. Even though I haven't used the "d" word, it's something to think about. I did write about suicide the other day. It was "fiction," of course and the character didn't have the stomach to do it, but it was concerning enough for me to seek out more help. I am unable to see that I might be depressed.

Acupuncture is no joke. I've always said a little bit goes a long way with me and Dr. B. brings out the big guns for my second session ten days later. Accelerated Energy (AE) Treatment will get rid of the "bad juju," she says.

The needles are placed in the Yin position, lightly, not too deep, to drain all the bad juju. Again, I succumb to a meditative place so rich, thoughts cannot form.

Floating in the center of the Earth, breathing lightly. How does the Earth's center feel? Solid, yet roomy. Supported on all sides by hot rock, but not burning. Supported in all directions—free to move and flow, to let go.

From the depths of no thoughts comes a memory.

Watsu.

I remember a lomi lomi training in Hawaii a few months before Lisa died. Earl, a Buddha-like man in shape and energy, waited with ripe juicy passionfruit for us when we emerged from the steamy underground lava tubes. We had released our "demons" in the heat of that sauna-like detox.

Later, I received from Earl a Watsu treatment—shiatsu in water—an earthy massage while floating. I trusted Earl when he drove me to a secluded pool in the Big Island rainforest. It was blissful and mostly the water held me, but Earl was right there supporting me even more.

According to Dr. B. the bad juju gets "exorcized" in this treatment. Red dots appear on my back; that's where negative energies leave my body. After a few treatments, the redness lessens, showing that the juju has been released.

When I arrive home, I feel weird like I am getting Afib. My heart isn't beating irregularly but it is a little faster. It seems to skip a beat every now and then. I am pissed. Acupuncture is supposed to help me, not cause AFib. Maybe it was just too much energy for me. Being pissed doesn't help the situation, so I start doing some yoga. First, I try alternate nostril breathing. Then I go down into a forward fold and let the blood rush into my head. After that, I gradually move into child's pose for a while. When I get up, it is gone. So what was that??

Afib/ not Afib?

Is the bad juju leaving me?

CHAPTER 35

Why Not Drum?

B efore Mexico, my friend Lynne had suggested I join her drum group. It was too much to think about then, so I didn't. On their Facebook posts, the Philly Batala group always looks like they are having a blast in their striking black, red, and white outfits. Their energy and smiles are electric and their rhythms hypnotic and alluring. I was curious.

When I return home from Mexico, she reaches out again. This time I say Yes. Because I am willing to try anything now. Since my usual "tools" for feeling better aren't working, maybe this will help. So I join a Samba Reggae marching performance band. Doesn't that sound like the perfect thing to raise my spirits?

It is late February, when I plunge into my first rehearsal, just a few weeks after starting acupuncture. When I look around the room, I see a diverse group of mostly females. Although the majority are younger than me, there are a few in my age group. All of them welcome me into the "family."

When the drumming begins, earplugs soften the blasting sounds and knee pads protect my knees from the giant bass drum that hangs from a belt and rests on them. The deep rich sound of the Surdo fills my body with healing vibrations. I am required to learn a variety of rhythmic patterns and choreography. Eventually I will get them, I hope. I'm decent with choreography usually, but who knows how my grief brain will do. Joy fills the room. The rhythms of four different drums blend. The pace quickens and explodes into a frenzy of sound and movement. Our leader is kind and full of life. I love it. There is a small monthly fee and the costs for gear and costume are reasonable, so I opt in.

I'm official.

There is a deep satisfaction, somewhat primal and tribal, that comes from the drum. The rhythms soothe me. And I have one of the best night's sleeps I've had in a long while.

The second rehearsal is more strenuous, but still fun. I probably shouldn't have done my booty exercises at home that morning. The extra lunges aren't helping. My legs are hurting, but somehow the vibration and the pounding of the drums take over and the discomfort goes away.

But the next day, every muscle in my body screams—a delayed reaction from me hitting harder that I ever had before. I can hardly move my arms.

As the weather warms up, we have an outdoor rehearsal on Broad Street. On this busy thoroughfare in South Philly, people are into it. Filming, stopping on the street, waving and honking from cars and bicycles. When we give joy, it comes back to us. We are the merrrymakers.

Soon after that I am invited to perform. I'm pretty confident when I stay in the back and follow someone, but have no clue how it will be when people are watching. It is more than a year since Suzanne's passing and I still suffer from a hazy murky brain that has trouble retaining information. The other more experienced players give good advice and tell us newbies not to worry about messing up.

St. Patrick's Day weekend in Philly is the backdrop for my first "performance," an impromptu "guerilla gig" at a couple of spots on the city streets. I'm excited.

Kelly green clad tipsy folk hear the rhythms as they approach and dance freely and spontaneously. An elderly couple carrying cello cases stops to do a partner swing dance. We are only a skeleton crew, with half a dozen of us, but we make big sounds and big joy. Our leader keeps it simple, repeating the same few patterns over and over. My grief brain appreciates that, as I gain more confidence.

The simple repetitive rhythms become hypnotic, almost primal, to players and dancers alike. There is freedom and safety for all, even without the drink.

Afterward, I feel like I've been hit by a truck from the physical effects of continuous drumming and carrying my giant Surdo around the city. Even though my hand is cramping up and muscles are aching, I still bask in the positive energy.

The next day I notice a big fat red bruise on my left leg, probably from not having the knee pad on the right spot. I'll have to work on that.

* * *

The next few weeks we work on perfecting rhythms and choreography. We practice, practice, practice. I try to remember the patterns, but they just don't stick in my head! I am still dependent on following other drummers.

Our next scheduled gig is more serious than the impromptu St. Patrick's street event. It's "Final Fridays" at the Philadelphia Museum of Art, an outdoor event that features local talent. We are to perform one 15-minute set at the top of the famous Rocky steps and another one at the back of the building

I'm building up my arm muscles and am figuring out a way to carry the giant drum and avoid bruises. I think I'm ready. I very much want to be ready.

Performance Day at the Museum in early spring greets us with a welcoming warmth. Flowering trees are in full bloom with brilliant pinks and whites. Violet crocuses and golden daffodils have pushed their way through the soil. As new life surrounds us, I am hopeful that the drum group will give me a fresh start.

But in the basement dressing room, as I change into the coveted colorful costume, anxiety begins to creep in. Perhaps my brain is interpreting excitement as fear. Maybe it is just fear. Maybe I should have taken half a beta-blocker (to slow the heartbeat) as I sometimes do before a vigorous dance class.

As the preparations continue and the excitement builds, I begin to feel light-headed and weak. My heart starts to beat faster. *Oh shit. What is happening to me? Stage fright? Panic Attack ? Afib? All of them?*

By the time we are in the elevator, heading up to the performance space, I am in full-blown panic attack. My heart is beating way too fast and I'm dizzy. I lean onto the elevator wall for support. I no longer feel like I am in my own body.

Because I am trying so hard to be okay and the show must go on, I choose not to say anything to anybody. And nobody notices anything wrong with me. *This will pass. I hope this will pass.* And now it becomes a prayer. *Please let it pass The set is only 15 minutes, I can get through it.* As I try to reassure myself, I realize that this is stage fright at its worst and now morphing into full-blown Afib with its irregular heartbeat. And my pills are in my purse downstairs in the dressing room. And yet, I carry on, knowing I will get through this. I have to. I am pushing my way through the soil and want very much to blossom.

There is nothing like the way time bends and extends when you are doing something that feels impossible. To make matters worse, our formation shifts when we spread out on the landing atop the Rocky steps. The person I usually follow is no longer in front of me. And from the back row, I can barely see our leader's hand signals. I will have to guess what I am supposed to play.

My inner being or my primal brain takes over and I make it through the set. The drum gets beaten and my feet and arms move, but I have no idea if I am in time or even what the heck I am playing.

Afterward, I inform everyone of my situation and decide to sit out the second set, spending a good hour or so in the empty basement classroom with the extra drums propped up against the walls. Street clothes and makeup bags are scattered around the room. In the stillness I realize I haven't eaten all day and haven't had much water.

I take an Uber home and it is a long night of terrible nausea. The entire episode lasts about seven hours until I finally fall asleep after midnight.

The next day when I call my cardiologist, he tells me to always be well-fed and hydrated, but I have already figured that one out. And he supports anything that I do to reduce stress, suggesting that I take half a beta-blocker before the next performance. Turns out my medication can be used to reduce stress. In fact, I remember Suzanne telling me that some people take these meds before public speaking. She would know.

After the agony of stage fright and the long night, I ponder my future with the group. Batala is a performance group, so that's what I will have to do. Is this too much adrenaline for me?

I also start thinking about therapy. Maybe I need more help. I am just five weeks into acupuncture. In fact, I was feeling "cured" having had no Afib episodes until now. I may have pushed too hard. And I am impatient.

In this second year of grief, I realize that adrenaline stresses my nervous system. I am teetering on a tightrope and any little wind might blow me to the ground. Without the shock and the distraction of the book project, all the uglies are showing up.

AND, I don't like them.

I research Afib, panic attacks, anxiety, and stage fright and get a hodge podge of different opinions which are overwhelming. There is a brain body connection, and I am trying to figure out how that works. My nervous system is out of whack because of the trauma of losing a child who suffered with the disease of addiction and ended her life by suicide. And my guilt is real.

I enjoy the band rehearsals, but it is performance pressure which causes my stage fright, so I start to be selective. In the name of conserving energy, I cancel my commitment to a 6:30 AM performance. And it gives me great pleasure to say NO to all four Batala parade events. They sound exhausting. If I can remain in the group and make choices about where I'll perform, it might work.

An early evening gig pops up and it seems perfect—a teachers' event at a local Marriott Hotel. I decide to do this one, but I don't give it a lot of weight. Who cares if I make a mistake? No one. I may or may not continue with the band. If it turns out not to be a right fit, I can leave and still be a perfectly fine human. And I can find another way to blossom.

CHAPTER 36

The Weepy Sessions

Meanwhile, back on the acupuncture table, I am weeping. It takes more than a month of sessions, but it happens. Turns out that acupuncture works as an excellent releasing tool. Gets out all the stuff that I've been holding in trying to be strong for everyone and wanting the world to know that I'm okay.

Also, I am flooded with positive memories. They come like little gifts. Here there is no place to go and nothing to do but receive them. Details emerge of the time Suzanne stayed with me before she moved to Dallas. Seeing the ancient turtle with the leaf on its back at the Philadelphia Zoo. The exhibit at the American Jewish Museum on Bernard Waber, author of *Lyle the Crocodile,* which I read to her when she was little. How we ate "vegan" at home for the month and Suzanne treated me to some vegan meals out at Charlie Was a Sinner and La Bombon. Our heartfelt tearful goodbye in the airport with lots of hugs and so many words of love.

The placement of the needles releases memories which help my body experience sweetness. Tears roll down my cheeks and then they just stop and I feel a little better.

My night sobbing in Mexico focused on Suzanne's ending and my regrets.

During acupuncture sessions I begin to go back in time to remember her life from before. This is where I begin to heal.

The bad news is that Dr. B is too expensive, and I will need to find a different practitioner.

The good news is when I break up with Dr. B, I find a place even closer to me and more affordable.

* * *

Spring, 2019

This weepy pattern continues at Healing Arts Community Acupuncture on Walnut Street, just a five-minute walk from my apartment. They have a a discount package if you buy four or six sessions. There are also several practitioners who utilize different styles of acupunture. Committed to this healing process, I decide to trust and let the experts do their work.

One time I have the sweet memory of my ex-husband's nickname for Suzanne. It's a long one: "Lubish T. McKrackin Whiskey Snapper Soda Cracker," which became Luby or Luby Loo for short. I hadn't thought about that in years. He did have a way with words! I remember us sitting at the kitchen table playing with Christmas toys before putting them under the tree—the Fisher Price xylophone and much later, Game Boy—I didn't want to let that one go.

There are more memories. Lisa's broken leg when she was two years old. It got caught under the backyard teeter-totter when she was riding with Suzanne. Suzanne may have felt to blame for that. She was so sensitive.

Suzanne in the library, having her meltdown because she doesn't want to leave. Scotchy, our golden retriever, as a puppy stealing socks from the laundry basket. And me chasing him around the living room trying to retrieve them, the girls finding this hilarious. Again, the tears run down my face.

There is another session where I go back almost 40 years to the details of Suzanne's crib—the bumper pads with their pastel blue and pink animals; the umbrella mobile, with little animals; the yellow and green wool blanket my mother knitted for her. Even her diapers—real cloth diapers and diaper pins and the diaper service that collected the dirty ones and left us the fresh clean ones.

How can the details be so fresh?

CHAPTER 37

Cheese Walk

As acupuncture begins to do its work, I prepare myself for the Batala teacher gig at the Marriott. I feel confident that this one will be easier, since I have some experience. I learned my lesson at the museum and take a half a beta-blocker in advance to slow my heartbeat. I've got this!

But as soon as I arrive, I feel a little off. *Oh this is nothing.* Denial is my chosen method. I reassure myself that all will be well. We are to be situated in a corner of the ballroom and provide happy, joyful rhythms for a procession of important teachers. Sounds easy. When the procession finishes, we are out of there! *Okay, I can do it!*

Everything shifts when last minute, we are asked to lead the procession. We will march, leading the important teachers down a long corridor into the ballroom. We will then reconfigure in the front and continue to play until everyone has entered.

March?

Not only am I new to the group but I have also rejected the events that require marching, like parades. Suddenly, I am afraid, because in our few rehearsals, we havent practiced marching. Our leader doesn't think of my lack of experience when she agrees to the change. Sure, I've carted the drum around the city, but not in synchronized steps while playing.

Ignoring my instincts not to march, I jump right in. We are about a dozen of us, in pairs of two, moving in rhythm down the narrow hallway. It's easy to march with a small snare drum, but the big ones take more practice.

Turns out that having a giant drum between your legs affects the way you walk. And I haven't yet learned how to adjust my body to keep in step with the pace of the other drummers.

I can't seem to take a big enough step forward, moving more sideward than forward, and I am beginning to panic. If that isn't enough stress, the giant drum unhooks itself from the belt around my waist and I have to fix it, making me fall even further behind. One by one, everyone passes me by. I am caught in a slow-motion dream sequence that becomes a nightmare. I just can't catch up. And that hall seems endless. When I start, I am mid-pack, but now I am the last one and beginning to feel like I'm in that awful game we played as kids, The Farmer in the Dell, where the remaining lonely Cheese stands alone. I am the Cheese with a drum sort of attached to my waist.

I will be the last one of the drummers to enter the ballroom. The teachers are behind me and the rest of Batala is probably getting into their formation in the front of the room. I can't see them, but I can hear them. I consider giving up—stepping to the side, letting the teachers enter without me.

What I want to do in that minute is rip off the drum, turn around and run back down that narrow hall *all the way, all the way home* like the last little piggy. In that moment, I want to be anywhere else but doing what I am doing.

I could have bolted. But I imagine the rest of the group is counting on me showing up at some point. And there are those teachers behind me. If I run or give up, I will upset the whole samba/reggae-special-teacher-procession pageantry of it. The show must go on.

So, I decide to do my solo Cheese Walk into the room. It is the biggest ballroom I have ever seen, packed to the brim with an audience and all their eyes are on me, this old woman with a drum between her legs, moving like an ancient tortoise, way way behind the rest of the group.

With a big smile, I enter the room as if that giant ocean gap between me and the other drummers is perfectly normal. This is a performance group, so I perform, but I am not smiling inside. Can anyone tell? The gap and the distance I have to walk solo feels like the distance between New York and California. It feels like the expanse explorers thought they had to sail before they dipped off the edge of the Earth. I might get scurvy before I reach the rest of them.

Determined and scared, I just keep moving, slow as it is. No one knows what else I am carrying besides the drum. I take the next step. Because sometimes that's all you can do when you are weighed down and don't know how to make yourself go forward any faster. You take that next step, even if it is a bit diagonal. because the path is not always clear and straight.

When I finally get to my place in the group, I turn around and fully take in the audience. They are standing and clapping to the rhythms. They are soaking in the electric energy of the band. Perhaps I am not that important?

But now I am feeling the fear again. What is that? Relief is what I should feel since I have made it across the ocean and instead of falling off the edge of the Earth, I have found land in the Batala group neatly arranged, moving to the rhythms. Stage fright has come back. I focus on the smiling faces in the audience and on Louisianne, the young French band member beside me, who is having a blast. I want to be like her, but I'm not. I'm having a panic attack. I try to pick up some of her energy, but I can't. I just want it to be over. It feels like torture.

Our five minute set feels like an eternity. My heart races. I am light-headed and zapped of energy. Afterwards in the hallway I feel relief. When the performance ends so does the panic.

But now I'm in Afib. This time I don't tell anyone. I just lean against the wall for support, then manage to pile into a car with some other band members to celebrate at a Vietnamese restaurant in Chinatown. I'm not missing the celebration! Sitting down, I am great. I appear to be normal. I even have a beer, some food and am semi-relaxed. This is the best time I've had with the group. One of the younger energetic members shares how she felt during a parade. "I thought I was going to die." Wow, it's not only me!

CHAPTER 38

Guilty

On the acupuncture table, all is quiet. I'm not pounding a drum or performing. In the stillness, I rest.

In one session, ambient background music becomes melodic and clear. I want to compose a song, but can't find the lyrics.

As background music fades, memories surface of listening to music on long drives. The trips to upstate rehabs and the Family School. Visiting Suzanne in Philadelphia. The road trip from Dallas to Denver with the majestic Rockies in the distance. I tried to rouse Suzanne from her slumber. I was trying to be positive about the move, but she wanted to sleep. And I didn't realize HOW very TIRED she must have been. So tired of her life. It's not that long ago, and I look at it again, as a witness from afar.

I weep. Tears cascade down my cheeks and down the sides of my face onto my neck, continuing down to the paper that covers the table. The thoughts fade and the music resumes. Lyrics takes shape in my head. Something about driving. Driving driving, driving… so much for the next new start. There were so many new starts.

It's so hard to love a person with addictions. I got angry, I took things personally.

In the end, all I could do was pray. I was powerless. Or was I?

And that's where the torment comes in.

I think about the guilt that I still have. *If I can only release the belief that I caused it.*

❊❊❊

"What's your support system like?" The question plagues me. I write it in my journal with the response. *Not good.* That's what comes to mind. It plays on repeat in my head. *Not good. Not good.* As I make a desperate attempt to be an energetic drum team member, I silently struggle with these thoughts.

"You are free, scot free," my good friend Ramona says, after Suzanne dies, but she doesn't know what it feels like to lose a child, to have a piece of your heart ripped out, leaving a crack. It is not freedom that I feel. Ramona is not helping me at all.

Great Silence has been my companion for all of this time. Should I offer an opinion, a tsunami of tears might accompany my words. A simple question, "How are you?" could unleash emotion which would prevent me from moving through my day. I become an excellent performer. I lie and say "I'm fine" to the question because if I make small talk, there will be more questions. *Do you have children? How many? Where are they now?*

I am angry and confused. I feel guilty. I remain quiet so that my feelings don't spill out inappropriately at a random person who just means well. Some people think I am unfriendly. I can't worry about it.

With family and close friends, I open a little, but not with acquaintances, strangers, and work friends. I don't broadcast Suzanne's passing to the world as I had done with Lisa's. The sadness was right there, but no guilt. None. It was an accident.

I am familiar with the uncomfortable energy shift, the pitying eyes, the confusion of a person not knowing what to say or do after you share, *I've lost my child.* As sad as it was, Lisa's was a simpler grief. Because Suzanne died by suicide, I have many conflicting feelings. It seems easier to just stay quiet.

I have become the best listener ever.

In the realm of Silence, I turn inward. Yoga and meditation soothe me. My writing and painting life expands. All the words I don't speak end up in notebooks. When I run out of words, I use brushstrokes and color. I layer sadness over anger over guilt on canvas.

Acupuncture helps, but the smallest thing can still set me off.

At the last minute, an afternoon model job switches to the evening. I suppose I could have said no, but it is for a teacher I like. Already downtown for a morning gig, with not enough time to go home in between, I'll have to hang out somewhere and buy food. I'd rather be home resting and eating my own food, but I am stuck in this weird time warp. Because my body is screaming no, and I'm ignoring it, I become anxious.

I read somewhere that depression is living in the past and anxiety is living in the future and wonder why I didn't say no to the nighttime class. I would have reduced a lot of stress and maybe I wouldn't have gotten Afib the next day.

I notice that strong emotion goes right to my heart and triggers Afib. How can I prevent reactivation of my sympathetic nervous system? That's what acupuncture is trying to balance out, but my system is pretty messed up. I realize that I must say NO to more things, and trust my gut. Listening to the gut is a practice I must work on.

In my self-study of Afib, I wonder if it has anything to do with repressed sadness, anger, guilt, fear, or all of the above. Or is it just chemicals and nerves? The brain and my thoughts can affect my body. That I'm sure of.

***

I watch an online interview with a therapist and his patient, a mother who has lost a son to suicide. Presented at the American Association of Suicidology's conference, they discuss "complicated grief." This is grief that doesn't get better over time, that comes with guilt and anxiety and depression. The trauma of suicide loss or loss of a child can contribute to this type of grief.

Even though the mother had made a pact with her therapist that she would call him if she felt suicidal, she doesn't. She made an attempt and survived. The therapist believes that suicide survivors, specifically, mothers who have lost children, are at a greater risk for suicide than other populations. I am not surprised by that. And in a strange way, I feel better knowing that I am not alone in these thoughts.

This client in the presentation says that because of her son's suicide, her own had become a possibility. Is that what happened to me? I am trying to feel better and make everything that I've gone through have some purpose. I know this—I don't want my life to be random. And that means I can't quit on it.

CHAPTER 39

Decisions

A few days after the Cheese Walk performance, I get a miserable cold, complete with stuffy nose and low energy. I start to *rethink* drumming. My friend Ramona says when I use the word *rethink* I have already made up my mind. She's right in this case.

Is my life better with the drumming or worse? So far, there's been a lot of stress management with me losing the battle. Instead of gleeful expression, the drum weighs me down, hinders my forward motion, and adds to the weight of my grief. I am already heavy with sadness and guilt.

I had hoped that this experience would feed my love for dancing, but the drum is in the way. As a tactile learner, I learn best when I throw myself into situations and experience them. And so I did. I want to have a new relationship with Suzanne. Drumming is not helping.

I have not forgotten the words of that younger band member at the Chinatown restaurant: "I thought I was going to die." Why would I need to continue to feel this way? I've never been a rock climber, mountain hiker, or marathon runner, like Suzanne. Suzanne would have thrived in the drum group.

I have lost my protective armor. I am vulnerable and my nervous system is out of wack. When I think about releasing myself from the drum group, I feel lighter.

Ramona says that drumming is the "methadone of face painting." She is right again. When I face painted, I had 14-hour days commuting from Philly to NYC. For ten years from April to October, I made that trip most weekends, even the first year after Suzanne died. Shock allowed me to do so many things without fully feeling them.

After 20 years of face painting, I have just stopped. This time of year is when the crazy busy season would begin. Going "cold turkey" into idle empty space feels too scary. So subconsciously, I wean myself off it with the energy of the drum group.

My friend Susan says after traumatic loss we get to do something *wacky*. After Lisa died, I "dated" half the men of Manhattan, many way younger than I. That was fun. After Suzanne, I joined a samba/reggae marching drum group and carried a heavy drum between my legs. Much less fun.

It is a hot humid May day when I send in my resignation to Batala. I donate all my gear—costume, belt, knee pads. I let it all go.

No One Will Care, Susan says when I tell her about leaving the drum group. *No One!!!* She says it with such force, I wonder if I should feel bad about it. But, I reject that idea in favor of freedom.

❋ ❋ ❋

Ramona had been my confident, my closest friend since she came into my life right after Lisa died. But now, 8 months after Suzanne's passing, and 18 years since we met, she is being sucked into a black hole of untruths and conspiracy theories. As I let the drum group go, I begin to realize that I am also losing my friend,

At first, she tells me how she goes on her "sites" late at night and how this makes her feel better. Then she shares some strange and disturbing Facebook posts.

"There is a Deep State," she says." RBG is dead "(she is not yet dead at this time). All these "opinions" shock me.

We have conversations where we find ourselves in disagreement, and I am left in astonishment. What follows these *discussions* are apologies, agreements to disagree, and expressions of our love. I am in no condition to navigate these crazy ideas, as she goes deeper and deeper into the abyss.

It is a politically polarizing time and the country is beginning to split. I hear about Q-Anon way before most people.

One day she posts on Facebook a pair of old sneakers or a painting of a bird and then the next day—boom—some reactionary post that creeps me out. I can't be exposed to this.

Reluctantly, I "unfollow" Ramona, beginning to distance myself from her. We have talked every day. About everything. But now I can't. Not only have I lost my child, but I am losing my close friend.

Ramona shares with me she that had been feeling "low" and posted about suicide on Facebook. I don't tell her that I unfollowed her and never saw the posts. We talk a little about suicide and she claims that she "saved" two people from killing themselves because she gave them permission to do it. I don't know about that. Some people don't consult with anyone. They just do it.

But now having this conversation, I feel more guilty that I didn't discuss suicide more bluntly with Suzanne. Ramona is telling me she handled suicide the *right* way, which of course makes my actions wrong.

In my journal, I write these words…

I want so much at this time to be free of the guilt. I want to release myself from blame. Because if I don't, I think I could die and I don't want to die,

I realize that Ramona is making things worse.

I read an article online that depresses me (never go online in search of medical advice!). It says that anxiety disorder can be inherited and a major crisis (like a child's sudden death) can bring it out. It explains that PTSD can follow a suicide and if not treated can become chronic.

I feel like I am in the chronic stage now. And wonder what to do.

What's your support system like?

Not great.

Getting worse because I am losing Ramona's support.

I make a decision to find a therapist.

CHAPTER 40

Grateful Not Grouchy

After a brief online search, I find my therapist, Cate, in a *Psychology Today* listing. I choose her because she has worked with PTSD in the military. And I feel like I've been through a war of sorts. So she should be able to handle me.

Even before our first meeting, I feel my body begin to relax. I don't have to do this alone.

Having Cate allows my shoulders to come down from my ears. It feels like a big sigh. It's time to talk about everything with no judgment. It's time to admit that I need more help. I feel lighter.

Her office space is modern and comfortable. You can write on the walls and then erase it. Cate writes all kinds of stuff on the walls when I speak. She takes notes and arranges them into themes and topics. She draws arrows connecting the related ones. I love this.

The next day I notice that I am feeling grateful for good coffee from La Columbe, an excellent choice of olives in DeBruno Bros, and my sweet little studio apartment in Center City, Philly. I adopt the "grateful, not grouchy" motto. Just having a strong positive experience creates more positive experiences. I feel more in control. Grateful, not grouchy. I want to keep that up.

On my second visit, I get her theory/ diagnosis of my current state. *Generalized anxiety disorder with notes of panic*—she describes it like a fine wine. How do I feel when I get the panic? she asks. "It's dread. impending doom."

Anxiety is an excess of unexpressed energy. Tears? Do they release anxiety? Is that why I always feel better after I cry? Sometimes exhausted, but always better.

In our next session Cate doesn't write anything. She just holds space because I tell her all of the memories I've had in a recent acupuncture session. All the times I felt "unseen" as a child, adding on those times I felt that way in my marriage. In this moment of deep listening, I am completely "seen." Sipped slowly, like a fine wine.

***

June, 2019

A few weeks after starting therapy, I head up to Kripalu to celebrate my 66th birthday. There I take a "Natural Voice" workshop which takes me out of my comfort zone and ultimately open me up to joyous vocal expression. However, the best part happens afterward, when there's no schedule and I slow down.

I had booked two extra days to just "be." And peaceful nature awaits. On this bright crisp sunny morning I cross the country road, and walk down the wooded path where songbirds serenade me. The short stroll takes me to the lake's glistening waters. With nothing else to do, I sit still and gaze. I go into a peaceful trance, noticing only how the light plays on the water. My eyes go fuzzy and I begin to see ripples of luminescence. With these new eyes, I notice the changing colors, dots of shimmer dancing on water. These eyes have been "Kripalufied," with the peace of no TV and very little phone time. My brain opens up in nature. My body softens.

A poem comes:

Reflective light specks

Amorphous watery blobs

like creatures moving

just above the murky bottom.

When the Kayak class paddles by, my young roommate waves. I return the gesture, feeling like a mother watching her daughter (we are the right ages for that). It's been a while since I have done this. I take it as a hello from Suzanne, who loved Kripalu. Just four years ago, she was here with me. The thought brings peace. As the Kayaks move on their journey around the lake, they grow smaller and quieter. The paddles all spin at different speeds, like pinwheels blowing on a watery lawn. Kayaking breaks the water with gentle soothing splashes. A few ducks follow behind.

Something feels different. *I woke up and felt joy without guilt,* I write in my journal.

Before this, I would wake up and initially think *I feel good* or *the day is beautiful* but then remind myself of Suzanne's passing and add a "but" to either of those sentences. My daughter is indeed gone from this world. It can also be true that the day is beautiful and that I feel good. I don't have to keep reminding myself to feel sad. Joy is my natural state. Somewhere in Kripalu after busting through the voice workshop and soaking up nature's beauty, I allow myself some moments to feel joy without guilt.

Amazing grace, how sweet the sound

That saved a wretch like me

I once was lost and now I'm found

Was blind but now, I'm free.

I add my own words to the song, something the workshop teacher would approve of.

After my time at Kripalu, I send a little note to Ramona saying that I haven't felt this good in a long time, maybe never. This respite has given me a jolt, a jump start, a fresh outlook.

Ramona does not respond.

***

When I return to Philly, the city seems harsh, noisy, and impersonal. At Kripalu phones aren't allowed in public places, so you greet people with your eyes, sometimes silently, but still with connection. City people on their phones are not available. We pack ourselves tightly onto buses and trains, avoiding eye contact.

When I get to my apartment it feels musty. The heaviness of my grief is palpable in the room. My space has not yet been Kripalufied. That will come later. Loud rock music playing in Trader Joe's and a screaming baby on a SEPTA train challenge my nervous system.

I continue to wake up feeling good and begin to think about releasing myself from a life sentence of guilt. I begin to believe that I am not responsible for Suzanne's death—I don't have that much power, never did. Wow, I'm not God and I can just feel good. It is a revelation to me.

Although I haven't completely embodied it yet, my thoughts are changing. Small steps. It's a decision that I must ultimately make, as I struggle to find balance

I feel so good, I start to think about a trip—something not at a Mexican beach! Perhaps something from the bucket list. Morocco!

Intrepid Travel has a two-week tour for a reasonable price. I picture myself on the camel ride depicted on the website. Travelers, in wrapped Berber head scarves, venturing out onto the sandy dunes of the Sahara, iconic long shadows beside them. The image entices me to sign up.

I invite everyone I know to join me on this tour. Ramona reminds me to invite Lorraine, who is the only one to say yes.

CHAPTER 41

The Rains

There's a change in the air, a shift. I feel my grouchiness melt away with the support of Cate, warm sunshine, and spring rains.

One day in June, as I ride the #9 bus down to the movies in Old City, the sky begins to darken. At my stop, I have two short blocks (a total of four minutes) to the theater. As I step off the bus directly into the downpour, my leopard umbrella serves only as a prop when thunderstorms drench me with sideways torrential rain. Clothes and feet get soaked through to the skin, shoes squishing through mammoth puddles that instantly appear. Only my head stays dry. By the time I get to the theater, I am dripping. I try unsuccessfully to squeeze water off the ends of my blouse while I wait in line. No one notices. I watch *Toni Morrison- The Pieces I am,* with wet clothes in a thankfully not too freezing theater.

Strangely, I don't mind the rain, I'm not grouchy. A few months ago, this drenching would have made me grouchy. But this rain feels sacred and cleansing.

Another June storm happens at night.

My student Chiara and I meet up at Time Bar for happy hour. She has just completed her English program with me at Berlitz Language School and soon she will be heading back to Italy. This is our first time socializing out of class. She looks beautiful when she arrives: a petite and delicate woman, with wavy brown hair and soft green eyes.

Chiara has been my student on and off for a couple of years, traveling between the US and Italy with two small children because of her husband's job. In our last class, something had changed. She seemed more confident, even powerful. She shared that her husband's been cheating and she will return to Italy with only her two children. I realized that her strong stature had come from her decision to leave, to put herself first. It was the right moment to tell her about my girls. Her eyes filled up with tears. She got it. She is a mom. Instantly, we crossed the line from student/ teacher to friends. I am sad to see her go and sad for her situation.

While we get tipsy from the Chardonnay, we talk about the major events in our lives and our ideas for the future. We laugh and we cry. Much is up in the air for both of us. Meanwhile, the sky has been darkening. We can feel the arrival of another storm. It is already inside us. Nature's release in not unlike our own.

We step outside into a furious thunderstorm. The sideways sheets of rain pelt us and create flash flooding that soaks our feet within minutes. Sansom Street becomes a lake. At some point we give into it and stop running. We surrender to the soaking.

We part after a few blocks. Chiara is sad and pissed. Anger gives us strength. It is life-affirming and motivating. Anger is better for forward movement than deep depression—I get that. We are not so different. In that last class, I told her how I was proud of her for claiming her power.

And then the rains.

The rain will purify, I keep hearing this in my head, because just like Chiara, my life has shifted. And I am ready for the change.

It's okay to feel joy. I let that sink in.

On my kitchen wall is a simple framed watercolor with a quote from a Taj Mahal song. My ex-husband and I had found it at a craft fair in Vermont in the 80's, our first weekend getaway after our kids were born. Everything about that weekend in Stowe was a disaster, but that's another story. I have kept this quote on a wall wherever I go to remind me.

Remember as a child

when morning smiled

It's time It's time It's time

You feel like that again.

As the month of June drenches me with rain, cracks open my voice at Kripalu, and slows me down, I feel fresh and new and hopeful.

***

When I write, "Will there be dancing?" on a friend's Facebook post, it appears to be an innocent remark. But it's so much more.

I had met Jen, a young French film maker in La Antigua, Guatemala while vacationing there in 2017, seven months before Suzanne died. I had invited Suzanne to come visit me there, but she was off rock climbing in Mexico with her boyfriend.

My time in Guatemala was one of my most social vacations. I befriended many young people who were studying with me at a Spanish language school. Every day there was a mid-morning break where we would all buy homemade snacks prepared by local women and sit on the lawn to get to know each other. I dragged some of them to the free dance classes the school offered and made them promise to meet me in the evenings for drinks, live music, and more dancing in this vibrant and buzzing little city.

I had started my solo travel in 2004, four years after Lisa died. The anticipation of the anniversary of her passing was always difficult, so I decided to leave the country for maximum distraction. I mostly traveled to Spanish-speaking countries for their affordability and dancing. I did tango in

Buenos Aires; flamenco in Grenada, Spain; and salsa in Oaxaca, Mexico. If I could dance on my vacation, I would be a happy traveler. In Guatemala, 17 years after Lisa's passing, I felt the most energetic and lively than I had felt in many years.

On dance nights in La Antigua, I'd walk on narrow sidewalks, hearing the pat pat pat of hands preparing tortillas for the evening meals. I would head to the city center where I'd have the daily special at the English Pub and listen to some live music. Then, I'd meet my young friends at a nearby venue that had live salsa music.

I became known for dancing with anyone who would show up. Sometimes our dance instructor would appear and I was thrilled when he spun me around the floor in elaborate combinations. But, I was just as comfortable following the repetitive basic steps of a beginner. "You don't have to do anything fancy," I'd tell them. "I'm happy just dancing."

So, this June, I see Jen's post where she said she'd be traveling to China.

And that's when I write that question, "Will there be dancing?" It would be a little joke, because of how dance-obsessed I may have seemed in Antigua. I had no shame. And Jen knew it.

I haven't made a light joke since Suzanne's passing. This feels new and different. It surprises me that I am able to remember the joy of that Guatemalan adventure and the innocent fun I had with my new young buddies. Without sadness or guilt.

I notice that I am beginning to break out of the Great Silence into the world of conversation. Small talk, jokes, even a simple chat without worrying about holding myself together. I know that it might not always be this way, but I feel a shift.

And In the same month I come upon this Hafiz poem...

The Simple Chat
*A burning coal against the flesh — who
has not felt this, from news that reached you,
or the shock to your nerves from bearing
eyewitness to horrific events?
The avalanches come, we should help dig
each other out.
The simple chat will return. May it last long,
and be realized as precious.*

I have lost both my children, suffering shock from their traumatic sudden deaths. How precious, I have come to understand, is the simple chat. To come to a place where heaviness is released and and lightness returns is precious. It is a gift to notice the little things — a chat, a sunrise, a hummingbird hovering above a flower, rippling water after a stone has been thrown into it.

June gives me this back. And the more lightness I feel, the more available I am to have that relationship with Suzanne as she is now.

CHAPTER 42

Rethinking Ramona

My inner world is looking brighter, but my friendship with Ramona is crashing down. And I can't go down with it.

A few months back, when I came into Manhattan for a show, we met for lunch in a midtown Asian restaurant. As I dived into my sushi, she threw out a theory—something about a sex ring in a pizza shop run by Hillary Clinton and Tom Hanks. I nearly choked on my food. I felt trapped. I was just trying to have a nice lunch with my friend. And then I get this crazy shit thrown at me. It was like she was possessed.

I wanted to run right out of the restaurant because a demon had taken over my friend. I took refuge in the restroom for a minute where I could breathe and remember that I was on planet Earth. I went back to my sushi, but it stuck in my throat. She continued from where she left off. I attempted to deal with each statement individually. I spoke calmly and used logic and reason to show how it didn't make sense. At moments I could almost sense a shift, as if she could see a flicker of reality, but then something else stronger in her brain would override the logic and she'd go right back into the weird zone. I couldn't get her out.

After that experience, I decided that I should just keep telling Ramona the truth and hope that she would come to her senses, but I began to notice that using factual information and logic upset her, as if I was attacking her core being and self-esteem. And I guess that's what happens when you get sucked into a cult.

Later I read a *Psychology Today* article, which describes how people in cults will not respond to logic. What they believe becomes part of their identity. What I observed was exactly that.

To add to the insanity is an anti-semitic bias in the theories, which I have been noticing for some months. There are times when I think that if we had lived during the time of Nazi, Germany, Ramona would have believed Hitler's dogma and turned me in to the Gestapo as a Jew. It's scary.

I begin to dread our phone calls.

In our final conversation, she admits that she's been following these theories for years and trusts that Trump will take down the sex rings. Wow. Once again I try to reason with her, even though it may be futile.

Afterward, she sends me an email, where she tells me that she has connected to my dead children and they have told her that I won't listen to her, because I am a bad listener. This email has now crossed a line that I cannot come back from. She is using my dead children to help support these theories. I am *rethinking Ramona.*

As she has become so entrenched in these beliefs, she tries to validate them using her psychic abilities. Any reputable psychic or medium would never do this—It is completely unprofessional. By countering her theories with truth, I have hit a nerve and she is lashing back at me.

The next day I have a full-blown Afib episode which I'm sure is triggered by the stress of our "discussion" from the day before. Finally starting to get myself balanced, I can't handle this chaos.

In an email I ask for a break for a few weeks to sort things out. She says she will check back in with me at the end of the summer, but she never does.

On that day, the last one in June, I begin to write this book.

CHAPTER 43

Not An Alien

A few weeks later I attend the Compassionate Friends Conference in Philly, just a short walk from home. A 50-year-old organization for bereaved parents and siblings, they have experience working with people like me. I remembered how helpful they were to me in NYC after Lisa died.

There I am the most comfortable I've been since Suzanne's passing because almost everyone has lost a child. There are workshops for specific topics: *suicide loss, drug addiction loss, complicated grief, multiple losses, stigmatized loss, single-parent grief, and no children remaining.* And I qualify for all of these groups. Wow.

When I look around, I realize that I am not an alien here, but one of them. The sessions are organized and professional. My brain just listens. My shoulders move down from my ears. I get hugs from the hugging booth. The freedom to just be me is such a strange feeling—almost unrecognizable. I start up conversations with other mothers everywhere, even in the bathroom. We walk around with big photo buttons of our children pinned to our clothes. I get a special first-timer's symbol and one for recent loss, which alerts other participants to be extra gentle with me.

And I meet a lot of interesting people who are working hard as advocates, especially for laws controlling medications and guns. I am inspired by these parents. They have taken their experiences and given their lives purpose. There's also a writing workshop and I attend that one too, because I know if all else fails, I will always have my writing. There's tons of information to absorb and processing to do afterward, but I am both validated and inspired. This is what support feels like. I sleep very well that weekend.

As I flip the calendar to August my old friend Anxiety comes for a visit. It is inevitable. Birthdays, anniversaries, and holidays bring back memories. As the second anniversary of Suzanne's death looms, I cannot shake the underlying uneasiness.

I space out and miss a model job. Out of nowhere! I am reassured by the model coordinator, that they know I'm dependable, but clearly, I am off.

To add to the stress, a summer storm causes my roof to leak. I place a row of bowls and pots in the middle of the room. The landlord does a Band-Aid fix. *Who needs this stress? Who wants to live in a place where you have to worry when it rains?*

Just before the anniversary, I meet up for happy hour with two of Suzanne's best friends, Lauren and Becca. I love them, but It is hard to be together because *someone* is missing. Two years seems like a long time, but we are all still raw. We hope to comfort each other.

Becca tries to keep it together by sitting with her arms wrapped around herself, but she cries quite a bit anyway. Her eldest son remembers Aunt Suzanne and how she used to buy him books. When Lauren presents me with a homemade quilt to honor Suzanne, I am overwhelmed. We are all suffering from loss, grief, and guilt and want our smiling, healthy Suzanne back.

We have some tough conversations discussing the specifics of Suzanne's suicide. At one point Becca asks me, "What is it that makes you not say, 'I've had it?'"

Little does she know how I felt in February, just seven months ago, my lowest point. I am not ready to reveal that beyond therapy.

I don't remember my response, but I do a lot of writing about it afterwards. I reflect on a recent interview with Stephen Colbert, who lost his father and two brothers when he was small. He said, his mother would not say, " Why me?" but rather, "Why not me?" Wow. Strong. That's how I feel.

So, why don't I give up? If I had not written that cafe suicide story, as a release from my complicated anger, guilt, and grief, maybe I would have given up. I got help and the help helps. In my deepest despair, I learned how a decision to "give up" can be sudden and reactive. In an instant, the feeling of hopelessness can take over.

I reflect on history—the Holocaust, wars, and slavery, and think of the many courageous people who survived terrible situations. Abraham Lincoln and Joe Biden lost two children. They didn't give up.

I think about the strength of my ancestors—my great-grandmother, my namesake, who had to run and hide from persecution in Eastern Europe, and managed to get all 11 of her children to Brooklyn. She didn't give up.

And my grandmother who lost a child in his early 20's to heart disease. Although they never talked about it, I remember my grandmother happy. She loved to tell a joke and walked to the local Y three times a week to play cards until her early 90's. She didn't give up.

I don't give up because deep down in my soul, I know I'm not finished. I haven't written all the books that are inside me. I haven't seen the Northern Lights or been to India and Nepal.

Life is precious and I don't want to waste it. There is sadness, but a twinge of excitement is bubbling up, for what will come next. I can feel it. The month of June gave me a taste.

Also, the world can still use me. There are plenty of ways that I can be involved and help my community and this country be a little bit better.

The words, "Never again is now," are spray painted on the side of a light pole that I pass every day. The world is changing and I feel some responsibility to society to speak out where I can and do my small part. Looking the other way is not an option.

I give myself pep talks in my journals by listing all the reasons to stay alive, and I am on my way to releasing the heaviness of grief. I know one day when another August comes around, my memories will be sweeter.

* * *

The anniversary comes and goes and I've made it through. In fact, it's been almost two months without an AFib episode. I can have anxiety without Afib. This gives me power.

A few weeks after seeing Suzanne's friends, I'm at a modeling gig, a five-hour seated portrait pose that allows for a meditative, relaxing day. Brain rest or brain wandering, whichever happens. Sometimes I compose poems in my head or choreograph dances. These pure daydreams bring calm.

Today I am working with a new teacher, new to me but not brand new, who is apologizing profusely for being late. *Hey, apologize to the students—it's less work time for me.* He puts on some music—a relaxing jazz mix, which meanders into pop into classic 50's and 60's country music—a nostalgic walk down memory lane.

As I begin to relax and settle into my meditative mood, I begin to wonder if this song mix will move me emotionally at some point. Boom! "Tears in Heaven" by Eric Clapton—the song that I associate with Suzanne's first suicide attempt, comes on. I feel like I've been ambushed, hit in the gut with a pang of guilt, and immediately I'm back in time, thinking how dysfunctional our house was. Directing the school play had been my escape from it—to my children's detriment.

My mind wanders to another Eric Clapton connection Suzanne had years later. The Manhattan halfway house she stayed in, after a stint in rehab, was also the same place Eric Clapton had gone to get sober. A plaque commemorates his time there. While she was there, she reconnected with her old boyfriend, used drugs again, and got kicked out. I feel a wave of deep sobbing just at the surface.

But it doesn't happen. I hold it in. Suck it up.

I am in a chair ground level within spitting distance of the students and they are drawing my portrait, so they are studying me. I do my best to not show on my face how I am feeling, but perhaps my face has its own ideas of what to do. I start to breathe more heavily. My loose clothing disguises the rise and fall of my chest. Can the students tell?

I consider asking the teacher to skip the song, but I don't think I can even speak.

Good thing it is a clothed pose. I am vulnerable, but not naked.

The next day, after writing about this modeling experience, I begin to feel shaky. I am doing laundry and having the "Day After" experience that I had read about in Mexico. At first I think it's a panic attack. I take half a beta-blocker to slow my heart, but it is too late. I'm in full blown Afib and my heart is beating so fast that I almost faint a couple of times. But, I am determined to finish the laundry, although I know that the physical activity of climbing three flights of stairs will make it worse. I have to sit down a few times while folding clothes in the basement's laundry room. On the last trip, I take a break at the bottom step to let my heart slow down.

All this from a song.

It is Suicide Awareness Week and specifically, Global Suicide Awareness Day, so I'm seeing more than a normal amount of postings on social media. There are many things that I'm not, but for sure, *I am aware.* Every time someone uses "committed suicide" instead of "died by suicide," I cringe. It is not a crime or a sin.

Clearly, there is more work to be done on myself and in the world.

CHAPTER 44

Support Group Shuffle

"Do yous ladies want them salads dressed?" the waitress asks with a perfect South Philly accent. Lauren and I are having a light meal before attending a suicide support group at Mercy Hospital.

We do. We want them salads dressed! We look at each other and smile.

Our waitress is a refreshing diversion from the reason we have come here—to find more help for our conflicting and overwhelming feelings about Suzanne's suicide.

Turns out that Philadelphia has a couple of these groups and I have already been to one in Center City, where I received a small blank notebook titled "Mental Health First Aid" complete with an attached set of sticky tabs. I guess I will be taking lots of important notes and will have to find them later with the tabs. The colors make me happy. That's a good start.

I'm not a fan of hospitals, but having Lauren with me makes the experience easier. There are a dozen or so folks from all walks of life sharing their stories.

I wonder what Suzanne must be thinking—her best friend and I at a support group meeting together? I'm pretty sure she'd be chuckling with us about our waitress.

Greeted warmly with smiles and kind eyes, I feel safe and supported at the meeting. A topic of conversation is the recent suicide of a local university director of Psych Services. And how fragile people are, even those who work in the field. His method of choice was jumping and I am keenly aware of how in a fit of anger or depression, a snap decision can be made. And then it is over.

Did he say "Oh shit" on the way down?

I return solo to the Center City group with my little notebook tucked in my purse. The leader hugs all of us. During the meeting, I bond with a young man, as he's lost his mom and I've lost my daughter so we are a natural pair. He walks me part way home.

Going to groups is hard, because everyone is hurting. Over the next few weeks and months, I find reasons not to go. Work makes me too tired. The time of the meeting is dinner time. The holidays are coming up and I'm getting ready for my Morocco trip, so I keep putting it off.

I also struggle with a few other groups—a women's "salon"in the neighborhood, and a group of Moms (who have lost children). Both have the potential for support.

The "salon" was an epic fail back in winter, with mostly younger women who had living children. Because of my situation (two dead ones), I am their worst nightmare, and my alien status returned. I couldn't leave fast enough. But, after attending the Compassionate Friends Conference, I was emboldened to give it another try a few months later. *What was I thinking?* I was so uncomfortable, I had a panic attack, and by the time I made the short walk home, it had morphed into AFib. *Clearly I am not ready for this type of group.*

And then there's Mom's Group. Created by Sharon, who had attended some of my grief workshops, she was able to gather a small group for regular get-togethers. Although I was invited to join, I resisted. The truth is these Moms knew before I did that I needed to be a participant more than a leader, but it was hard for me to take the step. It meant I had to let my guard down and be vulnerable with someone other than my therapist. And I am the only one in the group who doesn't have other children. I was scared.

Finally I get up the courage to go to a summer "meeting" at a bar on the top floor of The Four Seasons Hotel. I put on a dress, make-up, and earrings. We order fancy drinks at fancy prices. I like this format. The setting of the restaurant and the alcohol make it more cocktail party and less therapy. This group has possibilities.

***

September, 2019

I find myself deeply interested in the presidential primary race, so I say yes to an invitation from the Elizabeth Warren campaign to a debate watch party in a private apartment on Chestnut Street. A dozen people of various ages fit perfectly around the TV in the living room and there are refreshments. Before it begins, we are all encouraged to share our reasons for supporting Liz. It is early on and I'm not completely clear about my choice, but Nick, a young college student, is. He explains to everyone that he had come out of the "bubble" of his privileged community out west and had gone from conservative to becoming more open-minded about issues. I am impressed by this young Drexel student.

Turns out we are heading home in the same direction, so we walk together and talk the whole way. It's just a ten-minute walk to my place, another half block to his. By that time he has told me that he'd be volunteering in Nepal this winter and would be flying with his dad to Everest Base Camp.

We continue chatting at the bottom of the grey stone steps of my building. Soon it will be November, Suzanne's birthday month. Had she lived, she would be celebrating her 40th. I feel safe with Nick and tell him about my girls, adding that Suzanne had always wanted to hike to Everest Base Camp—it was one of her dreams. I am brought back to the first time she talked about it seriously—on the plane traveling to Tanzania.

And then I ask him.

I sense a certainty that can only be described as divine. I ask him if he wouldn't mind taking some of Suzanne's ashes to Base Camp."I'd be honored," he says without hesitation.

It turns out that a debate watch party is a surprise support group.

CHAPTER 45

Hello Darkness, my old Friend

With the arrival of autumn comes stress. Going back to work messes up my sleep because I worry about getting up super early. I'm also worried about the details of my Morocco trip. What is the perfect lightweight back pack and sleeping bag to bring? Trying to predict the weather in various locations in advance of the travel is making me crazy.

I am still new to the Mom's Group and not at all sure if it's helping me or hurting me. We have a Sunday afternoon meeting at Whole Foods. As I walk there, I react to the uncertainty. I feel myself begin to go into panic mode. My heart beats faster, and I'm light-headed. Suddenly I need to slow down my pace. It feels like I am carrying boulders in my purse.

There are two women there who are new to me. Using a derogatory tone, one of them talks about her late son's girlfriend as a "druggie." After that I don't hear much else. All I can think about is Suzanne and her drug use. I'm pissed. I feel like Suzanne and I have been personally attacked. It is possible that this woman is reacting to her pain, and has no intention of insulting me, but that's what happens.

I am the hyper-sensitive one, because even two years later, I often feel raw and vulnerable. And oh, it was so much better when I was in charge of the grief workshop because I didn't have to deal with any of this vulnerability shit.

At least I don't think about jumping out a window. So, progress?

Because I thought I was making substantial *progress* with my excellent growth in June, I had cut down my therapy appointments. I had forgotten and then remembered what I learned after Lisa died—that grief is not linear—it's an up and down affair.

What's the rush, Roberta?

The rush is I want to feel better. I'm sick of all this grief. The thing is I'm not there yet. And it can't be rushed.

Acupuncture still calms me down, so I continue the sessions.

Another day, I get Afib right before an evening dance class and I am pissed. *What the fuck?* Then I have two bad dreams that night.

In the first one, I shoot Suzanne in the face and she doesn't die. *That's not a dream—that's a nightmare.* I wake up sweating with my heart racing, but I manage to get back to sleep. Lisa's turn...

She is a kid going to school and talking about a soccer team. I ask her if she wants ballet lessons. No, she says. She also says no to voice lessons, but then on her way to school, it starts to rain and flood and she is covered in water and trying to swim out.

I wake up in a panic. Again my heart is pounding—I can't save her. I couldn't save either of them. In dreams and reality.

Anxiety has seeped into my dreams.

One October chilly night, I'm up at 1:30 AM and can't get back to sleep. I become obsessed with Suzanne's journals and can't stop thinking about them.

Later that morning I decide to bring them out and go back into her phone too. What am I searching for? Searching for the thing that's going to explain why she died? The message that's going to make me feel better? To settle everything? Or just curiosity? I can't rest until I read them again.

When I start to go through her texts, her phone dies. Not dies. Just loses power. A message from Suzanne?—don't go there!

But, I have the journals. I want to see what I missed or misremembered.

I hate you Dad

I hate you Mom

There it is again in black and white, technically blue and white. I think I had blocked out the word "hate" from my mind. I notice a downward spiral in her thoughts after she moved to Denver. Too much change? Up until the January before she moved, I was still on her gratitude list.

Oh yes, Suzanne kept lists. Gratitude lists and goal lists. A list of what she lost and what she had.

She was praying for *a calm mind* and *stable thoughts.*

I learn that it was after three therapy sessions in Denver, that she got the diagnosis of Complex PTSD. Around then she began quoting sections of *The Body Keeps the Score,* recommended by her therapist. She mentions abuse, but no details.

In her last week she wrote, "I can't stop taking tramadol." I hadn't remembered that at all. I don't even know what tramadol is, so I look it up. It's a narcotic. So how long was she taking it? Was it prescribed? I have so many new questions.

I am in deep now, so I go back to the autopsy report.

Chipped pink toenail polish... Puncture holes on extremities... 113 lbs.... Well- nourished.

Was she shooting up tramadol with the fentanyl at the very end, in addition to the gummies and alcohol? And there was Xanax she took before therapy sessions. Who knows what else?

It's amazing what she could put in her body and still be considered "well-nourished."

In her deepest soul, she must have wanted me to know everything. I'm sure she knew I'd be the one reading the journals. For years I'd saved my travel journals for her, but she never got to read them. Now, it is I who has to find my way through her journey.

My stomach churns with the details. And yet, I feel some sort of accomplishment that I am facing the truth, little by little, about how bad things were for her.

And I still don't want to jump out a window.

The looming holiday season, the trip planning, and the dive into the journals have given me a big fat red stress pimple on my chin. Who says you can't get pimples in your 60s?

I manage to steal away early in December for a few restful days at Kripalu where I do yoga, write, take wintry walks in the woods, and eat all my meals in the silent dining room looking out over the Berkshire Mountains. I luck out with no roommate and I dig deep into Kripalu's offering of peace.

But the blissful mood doesn't last. Anxiety begins to creep back in as soon as I leave the grounds. I have to wait in Lenox center for the Peter Pan Bus on a freezing day. At least I am not alone. My waiting buddy, also leaving Kripalu, is even more stressed than I am. She's brought papers to grade for the ride. Now, I'm calming her down. I want the calm to last.

It's a rough transition to home. The first night I wake at 3AM and can't get back to sleep. The next day, I do vigorous yoga and get Afib. After an hour long "bliss" yin yoga class online, I am back in my Kripalufied state. I write....

This deep inner space activated during meditation is truly the space between worlds. This blissful place gets us as close as we can to the Other Side. In this place, where time stops and we go out of our bodies, there is a heavenly feeling. I cried when I came out of it because I didn't want to lose the extraordinary state, and come back to my body and the world.

The world can seem so harsh. Gentle. Be gentle. I must remember that.

If our loved ones on the Other Side feel 10 times what that felt like or100 times, wow, well that is just impossible to know. What we can know is that we don't have to worry about them .

They are fine fine fine.

Even though I settle into a more relaxed feeling, there's an underlying nagging itch to go back into Suzanne's phone. I just can't sit in peace. I must continue my "search" for answers.

This time the phone stays alive. I am amazed at how she texted such ordinary and seemingly rational messages to people, like everything was normal, as she was preparing to kill herself.

We think that a person who is at the edge of suicide should look strung out. It's also possible that they feel some relief in their decision—a purpose, a way out of their pain. In their "haze" of getting themselves to the deed, their brain seems outwardly fine. Maybe that's the trick that the brain plays. Everything is planned out. And seems logical to the person.

In one text she tells Nikki, her friend who would be visiting that weekend, where the spare key is. She might be "sleeping" when she arrives early in the morning. Mully the dog will be "glad to see her." But, when Nikki arrives, Suzanne is already gone. Eventually, the cops have to break the door down to get in because she had deadbolted it from the inside. Why?

She tells her therapist that she'd be "out of town" Labor Day weekend, so she didn't make her next appointment. She'd reach out to him, she promised. When I contacted the therapist a couple of months after her passing, he was shocked and upset. Even he didn't have a clue.

And the awful text exchange with the current boyfriend who was breaking up with her, includes the mention of childhood abuse flashbacks, with no details. In the end, it looks like the break up was the final straw, but her journals show a gradual decline.

She writes lines that are almost impossible to read.

I'm unlovable.

I am unworthy

I am not normal.

I hate you Mom.

And now I sink back in the guilty place. And my stress pimple lives on.

Even though I know she is fine fine fine now, she sure wasn't then. And there are so many new questions. Good thing I still have Cate.

CHAPTER 46

Up and Down in Morocco

Morocco is "the trip of a lifetime," I write midway in the two-week tour. And we haven't even had the camel ride yet. All the stress was worth it!

A winding maze of shops in the Fez medina. Vibrant reds, blues, and greens of the handicrafts. Aromas of rich and savory spices. Tea and snacks in a remote Berber village. Tagines of lamb and chicken. Camel burgers. And cups and cups of sweet Moroccan tea poured from high above. Morocco is a sensory adventure that takes me out of my funk and into appreciating the wider world.

When I picture myself high atop a camel, I never imagine I'll be flat on my back on the sands of the Sahara. But that's what happens.

I never blame the camel.

Our camp is set at the edge of the desert, to preserve the dunes. It's a fancy glamp, with full plumbing. Platters of steamy meats, vegetables, and couscous are served to us while we rest on royal blue cushioned seats. We are promised two camel rides—a sunset ride and an optional sunrise ride. Both of course, please. Why not?

The sunset ride is perfect, just what I envisioned and maybe even better. We wear head scarves that we tie Berber style. In two groups of six camels, we venture out onto the sands. I am in awe of this giant beast with skinny legs who easily carries me. As the sun moves across the late afternoon cloudless sky, it casts the caravan's dark shadow. Tears come and I let them, while I am bumping around on the camel's back. The moment feels beyond beautiful. Spiritual—a gift from the Universe. I am filled with gratitude and appreciation that I can experience this vast desert that I have only read about and seen on film. I wish my girls were physically with me, yet I feel them close. No one can see my tears of awe.

"I am starting to come back to life after losing my daughter," I tell our guide Hassan while we are have a peaceful moment sitting on the dunes watching the sunset after our spectacular ride. The rest of the group has run ahead to a higher location and a few of them are rolling down the dunes like they are grassy hills. In this private moment with Hassan, I tell him about both my girls and he shares some of his personal life.

There will be another ride tomorrow.

I don't sleep much that night. It is pretty cold in the desert and my sleeping bag doesn't keep me warm enough. I get up when it is still dark to sit at the edge of the dwindling campfire, and gaze at the stars. The Universe is vast.

The morning ride up to the dunes goes seamlessly. We dismount but don't climb this time. The photos will be much better from ground level, with the dunes in the background.

We have gotten, perhaps a little too "relaxed" with saddling up, since this would be our fourth and final attempt. On our first ride, we were instructed to mount one by one, in an orderly fashion, while the camels were politely seated and waiting. Then, the handler would lead the first camel to stand up and the rest would follow, one by one. We lurch forward, then backward when our camels stand up.

But now, we were "experienced," so we thought. I have camel #2 in my group of six. One of our younger tour members, on camel #3, begins to mount before I am finished getting on mine. I have my left leg on the saddle and the right foot still on the ground. Without any prompting, Camel #3 starts to get up on his own and my camel just follows The handler is nowhere in sight.

It happens fast. I am thrown and land on my right shoulder, while my left leg splits before it follows the rest of my body. Immediately Lorraine is by my side, intuitively massaging my groin. Gina, a Canadian who is certified level 3 first aid, asks me questions and moves some of my body parts. With my eyes closed, I try to focus on relaxing fully to see what I really feel. I know I haven't broken anything. It's muscular, I'm certain, although there is deep pain. That is confirmed by the X-ray taken the next day in a local clinic.

241

It's a miracle that I haven't broken any bones and I haven't broken my glasses. Sand is not that soft when you crash down on it from atop a camel. And how lucky am I that Lorraine had switched to my camel group and that Gina was also there. Many angels and miracles help in this unfortunate mishap.

After being rescued by Hassan in the Jeep, and carried to the bathroom, I rest, trying to figure out how much pain I'm in. When I try to walk, I get the answer—a lot! I take out my phone and notice that it's Jan. 5th. I see a text with video from Nick, the young man who I befriended at the Philly debate watch party. The video shows Nick spreading Suzanne's ashes in the snow at Everest Base Camp! The wind takes them on a swirling journey. I am touched by this ceremony in the Himalayas. It's exactly what I need at this moment. And the timing! Not a coincidence.

Later, when I look at my photos of that morning's sunrise, with the majestic dunes in the background, I also see orange and pink orbs.. Are they my angel girls, in spirit, hovering about to help prevent my fall from being worse? I believe so.

I remember that I have brought some of Suzanne's ashes to Morocco. I had hoped to sprinkle them in the mountains, but I probably won't be doing much hiking. The Universe has other plans. So where will they end up?

***

One would think that being tossed off a camel far from home would be a horrible, unbearable situation. But no. The truth is I was in pain, but gracious love and kindness allowed me to transcend the circumstances, thrive, and enjoy the trip. Lorraine, other tour members, and the kind Moroccan people extended their hands and hearts and I felt soothed and supported. It is the most supported I have felt in a long while.

As I ride in the front seat of the van for comfort, our driver Jamal opens up the glove box and I see a pack of Camel Cigarettes. Of course.

After a few hours ride, I am "king's carried" from the van to a wheelchair that is waiting for me at a garden restaurant. Hassan and Jamal are on either side of me with their arms under the backs of my thighs. It's a tricky lift because of the location of my injury, a tear in the muscle connecting glute and hamstring. Even though it is extremely painful, I feel privileged and honored to be carried in this regal way.

From the table I am able to call my cardiologist to make sure it's okay to take the Advil that Lorraine has given me. (Gotta love the cell phone!) My butt is screaming but my appetite is unaffected by the fall. I am able enjoy my steamy aromatic plate of kefta (Moroccan meatballs).

There is a lot of carrying this day, including one "marriage carry," a solo carry by Connor, our resident young dare devil, who likes to show everyone his strength. For now,

I am happy for his ego and youthful stamina. He carries me by himself to the van which gives Hassan and Jamal a break from the "king's carry." Being "marriage carried" by a handsome young man eases my pain. I go limp in his willing arms and feel his compassion.

The concept of being carried as an adult, for any reason, is mind-altering, because for most of us, this hasn't happened since childhood. Seeing the world in the arms of another human shifts perspective. The world is different when effort is not needed. I have become the vulnerable baby in the care and trust of others. The result is feeling free and safe.

***

We head to the High Atlas Mountains for the next two nights, which will give me a chance to rest. The only problem is the 70 steps straight up to the mountaintop lodge. From the window of the van, I crane my neck to stare at them. It doesn't look promising.

However, our welcoming Berber hosts do not see this as a problem. Dressed in their traditional robes, wearing beards and turbans and big smiles, four of them transport me up the mountain on a pool lounge chair covered by a blanket. This is hard work and they stop a few times to rest. My eyes are closed most of the time because the jostling causes more pain and I am petrified that I will slide off this makeshift stretcher. When I open them, I can see kind and joyful faces. They use the blanket to hoist me to the bed. It's obvious they have done this before In these mountain villages, one helps without hesitation and with exuberant joy.

Helpless and vulnerable, I have no choice, but to receive their assistance. "Don't worry—be happy," one of them says to me. Tears form in my eyes.

I manage to fall asleep on my back, but wake up a few times to use the facilities. The bathroom is designed so you have to step down into it. This movement causes the worst pain. Lorraine and I turn a chair into a walker, and I slowly move from my bed to the bathroom entrance where I stop and stare at the step.

"I can't do it," I tell her.

"You can. It's only pain."

What? It's only pain??? Wow. What a concept.

So I take the step. It hurts like hell and I think I might faint. We repeat this every time nature calls. God bless Lorraine!

The next morning for my trip to the clinic, I am carried down the 70 steps and back up by my new open-hearted Berber friends. This time I am more relaxed and allow my eyes to see the cloudless blue skies and olive trees. I notice a mountain wall and palm trees on the opposite side of the road. The resident dog with wagging tail escorts me on the ride.

The rest of the tour group is hiking the mountains, while I happily stay in bed. The least amount of movement, the best. I need to heal.

Later when everyone is having dinner, there's a knock on my door. It is a tall Berber dressed in shiny royal blue robes with matching turban. He is holding my meal on a silver tray. First soup and bread. Then he comes back with couscous and chicken and a plate of tangerines for dessert. Lorraine brings me tea and massages my muscles with argon oil. I can't remember a time when I am so pampered. I am filled with gratitude.

In these two days I am able to put a little pressure on my left foot, now that I know I won't damage anything. And I find a way to walk by holding onto the wall and moving first toes, then heels, then toes, then heels. It is a little tap dance step that works to keep pressure off the injured area. It is slow and painful, but I get where I'm going— eventually. I will use this maneuver for the rest of the trip. In the mountain lodge, everything is close and the food is brought to me. I am sad to leave.

My caravan of carriers takes me down one last time. They go so fast, it feels as if they are running.

We are heading to an even higher place, and I will miss all the hikes with the views, but I don't mind. I am back to basics: food, water, bathroom, and sleep. There is a lot we take for granted, expecting our simple needs to be easily met!

The group is dropped at a lower location where they will hike to our lodging, a Berber home. Jamal drives me up a steep and windy road where I can see some of the scenery. I am "king's carried" a bit and then walk slowly up a few steps and down a long hall. My signature heels/toes move gets me to my room. Luckily the bathroom is not far.

This is not only the highest place we have visited but also the coldest. It is winter—Jan, 2020, and there is no heat. We gather in the dining room. Long couches hug the walls with their ornate embroidered white and red cushions and upholstery. There is a wood burning fire but I can't get as close as I'd like, because every step hurts. Shock has kept me going and now I'm exhausted. Hassan brings me a blanket and I'm grateful for the warmth. Platters of lamb, beef, vegetables, and couscous are spread out on long tables decorated with woven red fabric. And olives. There are always olives. Even at breakfast.

I am wiped out and have no problem sleeping on my back. One day I will be able to roll over without pain, but not tonight. I have my sleeping bag and am dressed in my thermals with lots of blankets on top but I can't warm up— probably because of the pain.

Experiencing physical pain has shifted my perspective and distracted me from any sadness that might seep in. Finding ways to move through the discomfort is challenging, but no one wants to send me home. I don't even think of it.

The next morning we leave for the coastal town of Essouria, and warmer temperatures. Hassan promises a steamy hammam (bath) experience with massage. He thinks it will "cure" me and I can't wait. I dream of warm water on my back and a big exhale, for I have been holding on tight. Also, we will be staying there a few nights and there will be a wheelchair available, so this is great—I won't be stuck in the room!

As we roll into seaside Essouria, my bones begin to warm up. We stay right in the medina and the streets buzz with shoppers and merchants. Unfortunately, the hotel has a long staircase to the second floor and a very long hallway, that I navigate with my heel/ toe move. I have my first shower and shampoo in six days and wash away the mustiness. Lorraine brings me dinner from a restaurant. Rested after a deep sleep, I make it to breakfast with a smooth toe/heel down the hallway. But going down the staircase is slow and painful. I rest for a minute after each step. We have a city "walking" tour that morning and Hassan will push me in the wheelchair. Before we leave, I want to use the bathroom in the hotel.

I am surprised to learn that there's no bathroom on the ground floor lobby. So it's back up the stairs for me. I stare at the staircase, having become intimately connected to its tiled pattern, and I realize that it's not going to move to accommodate me. I'm frustrated and angry and tired of the pain. Tears start to form in my eyes. I don't know if I will spit or cry. In the bathroom, a kind Moroccan cleaner, who doesn't speak any English, tells me with her eyes that she understands. I am touched by this wordless communication and feel her compassion. I have been holding on trying to be strong. But, on my way down, I burst into tears, then big fat ugly heaving sobs. How hard it was to do a simple thing like go to the bathroom. In that moment, I have a greater understanding of what it is like to be a person with disabilities.

When I make it back to the lobby I notice a few of the younger group members sitting on a couch. I'm certain everyone in the entire hotel—maybe even in the medina—must have heard me sobbing. They are studying their phones because that's what they do. I hobble over and sit opposite them. "I needed to get some emotion out," I say. They look up from their phones and stare at me as if I were an alien. They say nothing. There is a pause. Silence. I am waiting for a response, but it doesn't come. In unison, like a choreographed cartoon, their heads bow down to return to the important business on their phones.

Even at the time, I find this hilarious.

The next day is hammam day. After a short wheelchair ride and a long painful staircase, Lorraine and I arrive. It's a two-hour spa experience, which involves being scrubbed and bathed and then massaged. In a white tiled heated room, buckets of steamy hot water are poured over us. Immediately, my leg muscles relax. I lay down for the soaping up, but I can't roll over, so I sit on a chair for the washing. With a loufa, the attendant exfoliates every part of my body. I feel like I am losing years of old skin cells. When the hot steamy water is poured over me again, I relax more. After frigid desert and mountain nights, I need heat to get deep into my bones.

We enter a red lit room with soothing music. The massage starts with oils. When I am asked to turn over, my pain is excruciating. It takes three women to turn me over. Afterward, I feel refreshed and renewed. Hassan waits at the bottom of the stairs with the wheelchair.

We have a free morning the following day, so Lorraine pushes me around the local streets where we shop and have lunch before we get on a bus to Marrakech, our last tour stop. The wheelchair makes everything so much easier.

Our Marrakech hotel is the least accommodating, and the least compassionate. Too bad because we have three nights here. Our room seems miles away from the lobby and no wheelchair is provided, although every day, they promise to get one. And I am disappointed each day.

I miss the evening city tour. It takes me some time to figure out how to get room service to bring me food. On top of that, the room is freezing and I can't figure out how to turn off the air conditioner. There's absolutely no way I can climb over the tub to get into a warm shower. The deep washing of the Hammam will have to hold me for a while.

Lorraine and I taxi to the city center in the morning and find a horse-carriage tour through town. As the day goes on, I start to feel tired, like I am getting a cold. Missing the final group dinner and the "awards" presentations makes me feel lonely. It is the only time I feel sadness creeping into this vacation. I miss the friendly Berbers who brought me dinner on silver trays. Lorraine returns late with my "award" for "What Goes Up Must come Down," complete with a picture of a seated camel resting on the sand.

I am happy to leave Marrakech and return to Casablanca, our starting point, where living is easier for me. We stay at our sweet little hotel with a considerate and compassionate concierge. He remembers us and switches our room so it is closer to the elevator, and I get another warm shower.

It is almost time to leave this country and I still have Suzanne's ashes. After walking a little bit outside the hotel, Lorraine and I decide they should go in the park that is right across the street—the one with all the palm trees, near the Central Station. I am walking a little better now, but I am slow and it is still very painful. We have tea in a silver pot and pastry in the little cafe on the corner, like we did when we first arrived. Afterward, we try to cross the street that leads to the park, but the cars are whizzing by and I am afraid that I won't be able to walk fast enough to safely cross the road. So instead, we pick a tree right on the sidewalk in between our hotel and our little cafe. A short and sweet ceremony. So

Suzanne gets to Everest Base Camp and Casablanca. But I know she is everywhere.

CHAPTER 47

Reset

When I get home I think about the fact that with all that trauma and physical pain, I never had Afib or a panic attack. It must have something to do with feeling so supported by Lorraine and Hassan, and allowing myself to receive all the help that was offered. I feel so good emotionally, even with the physical pain, that my nervous system is starting to balance out.

In the two months of recovery, I set little goals, like walking a half block to the mailbox, then around the corner to a coffee shop. When I get to the coffee shop, I am so excited that I burst into tears. I tell the barista why I am crying and she gives me a free coffee to celebrate.

"You still using that thing?" the physical therapist says one day in reference to my cane. There is a point where a cane becomes a crutch and one can be too afraid to let it go. I take this comment as permission to walk without it. And so I do. Ari, my new barista friend buys me another coffee.

A few weeks later I start doing yin yoga in addition to the PT. Some of the poses are painful, but the slow breathing and the deep relaxation soothes me. Most of the time, since the fall, I don't feel sad or anxious. It's as if the body said, "Re-direct—we need you for deep healing. None of this emotional stuff!"

I write…

The body is a miraculous thing. There is that moment when you have to make up your mind if you want to live— not half live. Not live the gloomy, depressed, poor me life, but the proactive life where you care about yourself and have some passions in the world.

I knew after the accident that I wanted to live. And I am working my way back to that life every day. I feel hopeful, refreshed, and re-set as I head back to work in early March, 2020, with no idea of what will hit us next.

While I feel renewed and excited for what is ahead of me, my 92-year-old Mom takes a fall, breaks her hip, and needs surgery. What goes up must come down. I should know—I have the award for this.

On March 10, 2020, on my way to visit her in a Long Island rehab, I open a little bottle of hand sanitizer and some grains of sand spill out. This is very specific sand—Saharan sand, where I lay after being tossed by the camel. It has been just a few months, and even though I am much better, I still move slowly.

Oddly, my aunt, Mom's sister, is in the same rehab also recovering from hip surgery. My first cousins Roz and Lissy pick me up at the train station. This reunion is sweet—I don't get to see them much. It will be the last time I see my cousin Rozzy, alive.

Lockdown officially starts the next day and all facilities are closed to visitors so I can't see my Mom.

CHAPTER 48

The Plague

In the beginning it doesn't seem real. We have heard about China and then Italy, and when it comes to NYC, it hits hard. In fact, Queens becomes the epicenter of New York. The population density makes it a breeding ground for the rapid spread of the virus that we don't yet understand. Nurses use garbage bags as protective clothing, when supplies run out. Bodies begin to pile up in freezer trucks outside hospitals.

Everyone is horrified. The world is in shock. It is unbelievable, something you read about in books, but can't imagine living through.

Schools close. There's no meat or toilet paper in the supermarkets. Anxiety is palpable.

This is bad, really bad, I write in my journal.

I have a big fight with my mother on the phone because she won't wear her hearing aid. My retirement account is tanking and my work is getting cancelled.

I'm wiped.

When Mom is released from the sheltered bubble of rehab, she is healing well and able to walk and drive. But, she finds herself now with the rest of us, smack in the middle of the crazy pandemic, locked down in a totally different reality than the one she had been in. And it frightens her.

Caretaking from a distance, requires a positive front. But, inside I'm just as scared.

Mom doesn't turn on the TV because it's overwhelming. She would rather not know how bad things are. I arrange to have food delivered to her. Everyone in Queens is doing the same thing. To get food, you have to set up deliveries weeks in advance and hope for the best.

Nothing is as it was.

Mom regresses because of sadness and fear.

"I want to go back to the hospital. I want to be taken care of."

Stress affects her appetite. "I'm not hungry," she says. Who knows if she's drinking enough. Also she is disappointed with the food orders. Suddenly she doesn't enjoy an item that she originally requested. The local Y delivers her frozen meals, which she also dislikes. I pray…

Please please dear Lord God and any angels and guides out there. Get my mother the chicken she is dreaming about. And let it not be dry.

Mom is not adjusting to the challenges of the pandemic. It rips my heart out. My brother and I have to talk her off the ledge more than once. It is hard to see her this way. She's feeling nauseous. We tell her that she has to call 911 if she doesn't feel well in the middle of the night. "That's okay," she responds," I've lived long enough." Guilt, my old friend, comes calling. I've had enough of it and now it's compounded. I am fearful that I cannot take care of her well enough. *Will I let my mother die? Did I let Suzanne die?* I arrange for mom to have home care the next day. I also get a nurse to come and take her vitals.

Managing Mom from a different city is crazy and stressful—a retraumatization. I am reminded that I couldn't save my daughter and now I am trying to save my mom. Guilt speaks…

I killed my daughter and now I could kill my mom.

My brain goes wild as stress increases. If I send her back to the hospital, she could get the virus. If I don't, she could die in her chair. I do what I can. In addition to the home health aide, PT and OT also stop by for sessions. I arrange for house cleaning, so the apartment gets a fresh start.

Luckily, the co-op community also has some services for the aging, which include a very helpful social worker, and some nurses that call to check in with Mom and me. The social worker assures me that "They have eyes on Mom." But one of the nurses is more direct.

"Why don't you come and take care of your Mom?" she asks me.

"Because," I respond, "in 24 hours, we'd both be dead." I'm not sure if she finds this as funny as I mean it to be, but there is some truth there. I love my mom dearly, but in small doses. Now, I'm starting to feel guilty about that. The social worker always makes me feel better. "That nurse is probably not a good fit for you." You think?

A week or so later when my aunt is released from rehab, she comes home to a hospital bed and 24-hour care. She can no longer walk.

My aunt had been my mom's companion, her lunch and shopping buddy. They had done everything together. Mom feels more confused and depressed as she comes to realize that things may not go back to the way they were. My aunt's loss of mobility changes both of their futures considerably.

In a normal world, we would be thinking of a care facility for mom. But those places are death traps now.

It's a no win situation.

As I watch the number of deaths grow exponentially, I muse, *Soon I will have someone close to me die.*

Dear Suz,

Lauren wonders what you would have thought of all this and I didn't hesitate to say that you would be on the front lines, running into the "fire" to save lives because I know you would want to help as much as possible.

There is so much uncertainty. Mask or no mask? Vaccines and medications are just experiments in labs. All we know is the virus is spreading rapidly, large numbers of people are dying, and no one knows how to prevent or treat the disease. To make matters worse, our president minimizes it. *No big deal,* he says, but doctors and nurses are watching Covid attack people with a vengeance and kill them quickly.

That's how I lose my cousin.

CHAPTER 49

Sliding Downhill

Three weeks into April, Covid takes my first cousin Roz. Fast. A vulnerable cancer survivor, she goes into the hospital on Friday and is gone by Monday. It attacks her organs and shuts them down one by one. Suddenly, this pandemic gets serious for our family.

I try to be strong, but I ache inside. When I tell my mom the news by phone, she becomes distraught. Funerals are put on hold and everything feels unreal. It is as if we are watching ourselves in a horror movie.

When I speak to Roz's husband, he is angry. I get it—he has just lost his wife to something we cannot understand. We talk about how grief can affect the body. "My heart hurts," he tells me. I tell him about the dagger in my gut after Suzanne died. At this point, I am mostly numb and focus on managing my Mom which keeps me from falling apart.

The news gets worse and worse as the death count goes up and fear of catching the virus increases for everyone. We wear masks when we learn that Covid spreads from air droplets. The death of my cousin doesn't seem real, but the statistics on television are. I know I have to do everything possible to stay alive. I can't die. I feel hyper-responsible for Mom, since I have so much guilt about not being able to save Suzanne. It's too late to save my daughter, but I have a chance with my mom. So there will be no train rides for me for now.

Mom has help at home, but news of Roz's passing has affected her physically, as well as emotionally. Mid-May, she gets her wish to go back to the hospital, to an isolated section far away from Covid patients, to deal with gastro issues. Before she goes to the hospital, she says her goodbyes, like she won't be returning.

In the middle of everything, memories of Suzanne pop into my head. I think of our time in Africa— so very glad we took that trip. And how proud I was of her accomplishing her goal of reaching Kilimanjaro's summit. I remember her living with me in Philly before she moved to Denver and the sweet times we had in Philly. These pleasant thoughts give me a momentary respite from sickness and death.

Since I can't be with Mom in the hospital, I call upon Nurse Suzanne, to keep an extra eye out for her. Because Mom is not really sick—just backed up—she enjoys all the attention from doctors and nurses. I feel relieved that she is safe and in good hands. I have my best sleep in months.

A week in the hospital turns out to be exactly what she needs. There's a burst of energy when she gets home—a shower, a cleaning of the refrigerator, a conversation with her pharmacist to update and refill needed meds. A desire to go to the bank drive-thru. "I made up my mind," she states. She is choosing life over depression. And I am inspired by this.

When there's a little break in the Covid severity, she is thrilled to go back to driving and shopping and carrying her packages up the stairs. With mom in a better frame of mind, I can focus more on me.

I am grateful for my health. For breath. For the sun and the flowers. For the fact that my mom chooses life. In this crazy time of loss we celebrate little things and take nothing for granted.

But Covid has affected everything. My work just stops. Pretty much all of it. Complicated paperwork must be submitted to receive the special pandemic unemployment. As a freelancer, we are not typically eligible for unemployment, so this is good news. I work hours on the application with questionable success. My application is returned to me several times, for more information. As a result my checks are delayed. We don't know how long the pandemic will last. Uncertainty causes more stress. Who knows if any of my work will ever come back?

I walk the desolate Philly streets in search of normalcy. Always masked, I keep a six-foot distance from other people. If I see an unmasked person, I move even further away, or maybe even cross the street. I become acquainted with stately oaks, mottled sycamores, and flowering azaleas. Window boxes are bursting with pink and red impatiens and dripping verdant vines. I notice houses with doors painted purple and blue. Giant ceramic pots filled with fragrant roses decorate the sidewalks. As I brush against them, a sweet scent fills the air. There is life and color, even in the midst of so much death. Maybe it was always this way, but I hadn't time to notice. Maybe it is just a little bit more vibrant because it's something we can do.

I meander down historic narrow streets of Belgian block and cobblestone. My urban "forest" lets me escape from the confinement of my home. Deep in reverie, I'm not paying attention to the uneven terrain when I roll my foot while sloshing around in unsupportive sandals and now have an injury. There is swelling and fiery pain.

I hobble around for some days, taking Tylenol, which doesn't work. Sitting makes me crazy. So I take a leap and go for acupuncture where I must have my temperature taken, use hand sanitizer, and wear a mask. Miraculously, the pain is drained from my foot. I can actually feel it leaving. Acupuncture has served me well for emotional and stress issues. But this is the first time I've ever come for physical pain. And it's magic. After a few more sessions and some massage, the swelling goes down and I can resume stomping around the hood.

CHAPTER 50

We Do What De Can Do

I'm going to sleep, so I can live.

Suzanne says this in a dream, which wakes me up only 90 minutes after I've fallen asleep. I always check the time when I wake up on my old-fashioned battery operated analog clock with its round white face and black rim. Usually, without my glasses, I get it wrong. This dream jolts me into a heart-pounding wakefulness, so I am certain of the time. The dream…

I have a big sit down with Suzanne and tell her that I am concerned about her drinking. Then she disappears and I worry. When she returns, her face is dirty and she has a bruise over her right eye. "What happened?" I ask her. She is in full blown relapse mode and my body feels it, the same way I felt it when she told me that she thought she could start drinking again back in 2014. "I'm going to sleep so I can live," she tells me.

Panic wakes me up. It is so real.

I'm going to sleep so I can live.

What does that mean? Is Suzanne giving me a reason for her suicide? I know that now she is free from mental anguish and addictions. She lives on in her perfect spirit. And I am starting to get glimpses of how her new "life" and mine connect.

I sign up for some Zoom art classes, including botanical drawing, something I've never done. The teacher has us shading by lightly drawing tiny circles with soft pencils. Over and over, we layer more squiggly circles to get the shading correct. I have never done such light and slow detailed work. I've been more of the bright colors, abstract, throw paint kind of person. But there's something soothing about drawing tiny circles and watching a leaf form or an apple appear gradually over time.

Drawing repetitive tiny circles calms me. There's a meditative quality to it. It is something I can do while waiting on hold to find out what the heck happened to my unemployment checks. It is something that I can do while dealing with my landlord's inability to permanently fix my leaking roof, as we experience heavy rainstorm after rainstorm. It is something that gets me through the stress of having my identity stolen. As layers of the pandemic build, so do the circles, but with very different results.

In the midst of uncertainty, layer upon layer of tiny circles becomes something—a leaf or a flower or a piece of fruit. With the pandemic, life just keeps going with new challenges after new challenges. What is similar is uncertainty. This slow drawing of botanicals tests one's patience. It cannot be too slow because, like all life, the green leaf or the ripe apple changes. An edge curls or brown spots appear. One cannot be too slow or the appearance will be too different. The fruit will rot and smell and need to be thrown away. Nothing lasts forever. What lives must also die.

In midsummer, Mom is still riding high on her rebirth and my unemployment checks start to appear. As a result, I have my own energy burst and begin to organize my place. I buy a new bookcase and put it together myself. I purchase a new storage ottoman for my writing notebooks. I clean out and re-arrange my drawers. Underneath a stack of sheets I find buried treasure—a card from Suzanne written in 2014 after her wedding.

Dear Mama (officiant, DJ, therapist, etc),

Thank you for being so amazing throughout this wedding planning craziness. Thank you for being our officiant. And most of all, thank you for being my mom. I only hope this card makes you feel half as warm and cozy as you have made me feel to be your daughter.

So much love,

Suz

Thank you Suzanne, for these words of love. Received at exactly the perfect time. How did you know? Suzanne is very much alive in this message. *So, Suz, this is how it's going to be with you and me. I like this.*

As my summer Zoom art and writing classes come to completion, Philly art schools are trying to figure out how they will use models. I have pretty much decided that I won't go back to work and into an art classroom unless I am completely surrounded by plexiglass and everyone is wearing a mask. That won't happen.

Emergency alerts go out in the Philadelphia area—a hurricane is expected, with tornado warnings. People are encouraged to take shelter in their basements as roofs will blow off.

And my roof still hasn't been properly repaired. I'm scared.

As expected, a deluge pounds on the roof while I stand guard watching for cracks. So far so good. I am at my writing table finishing up a botanical watercolor. A new spot leaks—little drips begin to fall on me. Oddly refreshing. Soon there are four mixing bowls and a baking pan stretched across my room catching more rain. The force with which it falls causes splatter and my carpet dampens in between the bowls. That's when the towels come out. I notice the ceiling bubbling up in new places. The drips over my chair are slow and I am just letting them happen, but when I notice that my printer is also getting wet, bowl number five goes there. The musical pings and dings sound in various notes of the musical scale—not the concert I was hoping to attend.

The next day, I make numerous calls to maintenance and roofers. Promises are made to take care of this, but none of the little Band-Aids work. This can't continue.

Online therapy and acupuncture help. The acupuncture session is a weepy one, as I realize that it will soon be Suzanne's anniversary. My roof is crying too.

As I become more annoyed, the calls become heated. "Look lady—you have a problem with the rental company!" the irritated roofer says to me. My throat tightens and my polite tone disappears. I yell into the phone. "I have a name and don't want to be called 'Lady'!" He hangs up. Cell phone hang ups are so anticlimactic—just dead air. You can't tell if the person is there or not. Not like the old days when you could slam down a phone and make some noise. If I had my old yellow rotary wall-phone, and he slammed his phone down on me, I would have slammed mine back. There was some satisfaction in the physical action of slamming down the phone.

I am done. "This apartment is unlivable," I tell the rental company. "If it's not fixed, I'm moving!" I say it forcefully but calmly. I have arrived at my breaking point. I think the word "unlivable" triggers the response. They send over a kindly older man, someone whom I have never met, probably reserved for these kinds of sticky situations, and we bond. He hears me. And he sees the problem with his own eyes. For the first time, I feel like my rights as a tenant have been respected. He will recommend a new roof. And a temporary fix until that happens, as we have a forecast for five days of heavy rain. Can I trust him?

After our meeting, I step outside where thick humidity and poor air quality punch me in the face. This triggers a strong physical reaction—a panic attack—lightheadedness and shortness of breath. I can't feel safe in my apartment, and with Covid still around, I don't feel safe outside either. I continue on, determined to find a cup of coffee and sit in the park, but the bad feelings don't let up, even after taking a beta-blocker. Not until I arrive back home and turn on the air conditioner, do I find some relief.

CHAPTER 51

Elevated

"Caution! Bus is turning. Caution! Bus is turning."

I hear this over and over as I receive a much-needed massage from my dear friend, Jen. I am trying everything I can to deal with my stress.

Her office sits a block from the busy thoroughfare of Germantown Avenue and the nearby #23 bus stop. The bus runs frequently and plays the recorded warning often.

Jen uses warm oil, a woodland fragrance, and calming music. As I sink into the table and relax to soothing touch, my mind wanders. From the open window, I feel a gentle breeze and hear the words. "Caution! Bus is turning." It is not jarring. The words float, infused into the meditative mix like a musical refrain. The repetition feels like a specific message for the moment.

We go along feeling okay. We are calm, at peace But the bus is always turning. A child dies. Then another. A pandemic. A hurricane. A leaking roof.

Don't get complacent.

Caution, Bus is turning!

"I am just beginning to come out of the fog of grief," I tell Woody, Roz's husband, as I acknowledge her birthday. It will be three years end of August since Suzanne's passing.

I let myself listen to one of our car songs—the Joan Baez/ Dar Williams version of "You're Aging Well." Suzanne and I used to sing it together on rides to and from the Family School. I weep as I listen. It was for us a song about overcoming struggle. Those were the hopeful days and moments of closeness that I treasure. How am I aging today?

Dear Suzanne and Lisa,

Was it really you guys in the dream last night? What if our whole family can meet up in a dream? It was perfect— in a water park—we always loved amusement parks as a family. And so nice to see you running into our arms after the ride. And to feel you! It seemed like you missed us so much.

Suzanne, as your anniversary approaches, I find myself weepier. I keep looking for ways to have saved you. I think where you are right now, you understand everything. I am still trying to figure it out.

You two were and still are beautiful souls who cared about others and wanted to help. I miss your hearts. Come and visit me any time you want.

Love,

Momsy

* * *

My young friend, Nick (of the ashes), stops in Philly for a meal with me and we dine al fresco. Afterward, I start to worry about catching the virus. I have not had close contact with anyone and Nick had just gotten off a plane, where bad germs could be lurking. Even though we were outside, I'm still traumatized by the loss of my cousin and the terrible statistics. All week I've been swallowing a lot, thinking I have a sore throat. Any little throat tickle, it must be Covid. Sneezing? Covid. Chest pain? Covid. I wake up tired from worrying.

My therapist says I am "elevated," on edge, partly because of Suzanne's looming anniversary. It is a strange word, "elevated." It seems positive, like I've moved up, gotten extra points, reached a higher spiritual calling, rank, or degree. But, no. It means my normal grounding is missing. I am in a sense off-ground, above ground, free floating in air, trying to find some connection to the Earth, but instead I can't touch it.

"I want to exhale," I tell Cate, "but I can't." I could die of Covid. Also, we might be losing our democracy. There are so many layers of stress.

Elevated. "Caution! Bus is turning."

CHAPTER 52

Necessary Adjustments

S eptember starts with a new roof that seems to be holding. The light has shifted and we are having cooler temperatures. If you look at Center City, you wouldn't know that we were in a pandemic. We are now in the "streetery" phase, where restaurants have built little shelters for outdoor seating so customers don't have to be in "superspreader" environments with potential death germs floating around. If you look closer, you will notice masked pedestrians. The masks reveal that the pandemic is still with us. Masks have become normal, even essential.

And there are new challenges.

Most schools have gone online, but enough college students have returned to the city to give it more life. I'm hired for an 11-session online model gig for an art school which requires a big step out of my technical comfort zone. During an online "training," I have a panic attack, which turns into Afib. On the instructed days, I tune into the teacher's Zoom and am just one of the participants. I will be "pinned" so they can focus on my pose. The instructed days are easy as the teacher lectures quite a bit. I turn off my camera until she needs me and use this free time to get a lot done. This is not so bad.

Included in the course are optional uninstructed modeling sessions. For these I'm on my own. I must create a YouTube live event, which scares the hell out of me, but I figure it out. I pose on my bed in a red sundress with colorful sarongs draped underneath and around me. Although students are supposed to be painting, I don't see them or even hear from them, unless someone writes a comment. No one ever does. I pose for empty air. It is the loneliest job I have ever had.

Another unexpected annoyance happens when I go to the bank to get quarters for my laundry. They are out. The banker tells me they haven't gotten any new coins in two months. How strange? Now, with every monetary exchange, I attempt to get a couple of dollars in quarters so I can have clean clothes. I get the most quarters at the farmers' market. They know me for that, now.

Also, my mother is beginning to worry about forgetting things. She calls me on the phone and blurts out everything she needs to tell me as fast as she can, so she doesn't forget something. She is worried about it. "I feel like there's something I've forgotten," she says at the end of every call. I tell her if it's important she can call me later. I talk about coming to visit her—"I'll lock the doors!" she says. She is still worried about me catching Covid, like her niece Roz did. I am worried too.

She tells me over and over again to "Be careful." I am as careful as possible. I don't think she fully understands that when I say I'm taking an art class or modeling or "going" to a concert, that it's happening online in my apartment and I'm not going out into the world.

We do what we can.

I start making phone calls for the election. "I will crawl on cut glass to make sure my ballot gets turned in," I tell someone. As my fears about our country increase, volunteering makes me feel better. Calling the middle of the state of Pennsylvania is not for the weak-hearted. People are grouchy and they sometimes yell at you. *Take nothing personally,* is the mantra. There are only two months until the election and I'm all in.

Mid-September on a bench in Rittenhouse Square, I'm dressed in a sweater, long pants, socks and boots. Some city dwellers, refusing to let go of summer, strut past me in shorts and sandals. It is noon and the church bells chime. They mix with the triplets of a trumpeter on the opposite side of the park. Drilling is taking place on the street south of the park and car horns honk. The sounds layer upon each other like a finely composed symphony Though not melodic, they mix and blend and you can imagine a conductor pointing his baton to each musician.

All at once the bells go silent. The drilling quiets and only the lone trumpeter can be heard. But not for long. The imaginary Maestro points to the drilling section and they begin. He points to a lawn mower and its roaring engine blends in. The wind section is called upon to swirl around some dry brown fallen leaves and there's a scratching sound. A pair of footsteps crunches on them when they hit the pavement.

I have been weepy these last mornings. Maybe it's the slant of the light that reminds me of Suzanne's memorial which we had around this time three years ago. Maybe it's the looming 20th anniversary of Lisa's passing. I mourn the loss of Ruth Bader Ginsburg and John Lewis, two of my heroes. The world has lost some purity.

One day while I'm phone banking, a person goes ballistic on me and starts cursing. He gets pissed off when I tell him that what he thinks is a ballot is probably an application for one because the ballots have not yet been sent out. He gets so nasty, I have to hang up and run out of the house. So much for the mantra *Take Nothing Personally.*

As the chill sets in, I wonder what will keep me busy after the election. What will distract me from the sadness that remains underneath? No trip to look forward to. No Kripalu. Those things have helped.

What would RBG do? She'd get to work. What would John Lewis do? He'd get back to work. Hillary Clinton, after losing the election, took long walks in the woods and went to Broadway musicals. Then she went back to work. And so, I'll let the tears flow for now and when they dry, I'll get back to work.

I step up my volunteering for the election by taking on a role with Voter Protection. This forces me (masked of course) out of the house to assist with live people waiting on real lines for early voting at various locations around the city. City Hall is the closest to me, but I choose a bunch of shifts at the Liacouras Center on the Temple Campus in honor of Suzanne. On my first shift, my partner is a nurse (like Suzanne was). I find out that her husband is a nurse at Jefferson (where Suzanne worked) and he may have known her. Each time I go, I feel like I am making pilgrimage to her memory. I remember how she led the double life of student/AA member; how she invited me to sleep over in the dorms her freshman year; and how she returned here triumphantly to graduate after her first relapse. As I run up and down the long lines of voters, answering their questions, I notice Rock Hall directly across the street. This is where Suzanne performed in concerts. When I pause for a moment, her sweet voice plays in my head and I have to fight back tears. This is the Suzanne I want to remember.

A dream...

We are preparing for a tap dance recital. But I have figured out a way to fly in the air with my tap shoes. I just jump. And then I stay there, defying gravity. I float around corners and through doors. Everyone is busy getting dressed, applying makeup and fixing their hair. No one thinks it strange that I hover above, sailing weightless.

In this dream there is no stress. Just freedom. In so many other dreams, I am lost or worried. This dream feels like a gift.

CHAPTER 53

After the Election

W hen my election volunteer work ends, there's a huge void. A vast sea of Nothing with an indiscernible horizon. Nothing. Nothing. Nothing. As the virus spreads again, I feel more restrictions coming on. Best to stay home.

We do what we can do. Making plans is impossible. I bring out the paints and mix a black from cobalt blue and a burnt sienna. I am thrilled with the color. This color fills in some of the empty space around me. Returning to painting, is something I can do.

I discover smoked turkey necks at the supermarket one day, which I start adding to my slow cooked soups. Smoked turkey necks excite me almost as much as the black I mixed. It is my new culinary pleasure. The apartment fills up with the aroma of smoked meat.

When I sleep, the girls visit. The dream…

Lisa is wearing high heels, two-tone, black and white. I thought we were going hiking so I ask her if she has other shoes. Suzanne wants to sleep, and Lisa says she has to go to rehearsal at 12PM. Suzanne was going to take her, but she wants to sleep. I ask Lisa where it is and she says, "It's a couple hours away, in the South Seas". Then she laughs and tells me, "The high school!" She keeps asking if there are any boys for some of the small roles—a little talking, a little singing. I think one of Suzanne's boyfriends may be available, but she wants to sleep and I let her.

Suzanne was so tired at the end of her life. Letting her sleep seems logical.

I have to sleep so I can live.

I wake up to more Nothing. It's late November, bleak and chilly and I don't want to be outside. Although my girls show up in my dreams, the silence and stillness of the day is overwhelming. It is a good time to go deep within and just be.

Pandemic Thanksgiving is strange and lonely. Sharon invites me to a vegan feast at her place, but I'm still afraid of close contact in groups, so I decline. I begin to bake—mostly muffins with honey and dried fruit—and share with my neighbors. At DeBruno's I buy some prepared foods: turkey with gravy, sausage stuffing, and cranberry sauce. I have my own private celebration with homemade corn muffins, a glass of Prosecco, and some Netflix.

In a weepy session with Cate, I tell her the history of my oak kitchen table, which now serves as an "everything table" in my studio apartment. When my kids were young it was the "art table," where we made Play-Doh creations, glittery Valentine hearts, finger paintings, and of course, cookies. I decide to fill up the endless time with more baking. And to revive Cookie Day!

When Lisa died, the holidays were so gloomy and Suzanne and I found it impossible to do holiday shopping. We created Cookie Day, in honor of Lisa, to bake and send tins of the sweet treats to our family and friends.

Cookie Day evolved into Cookie Weekend and when I moved to Philly, it got even bigger. We invited friends to eat and bake with us. I started making soup and it became a party—Cookie Marathon. Suzanne always got the tins. We dealt with long lines at the post office snd one year Suzanne broke open a tin and shared the yummies with other weary customers—I wonder who didn't get their cookies that year?

One year when the main post office moved, we couldn't find it. Frustrated, we wandered around the desolate industrial wasteland of Market Street near 30th Street on a cold and windy day with garbage bags of filled cookie tins. We never found it, but we were not going to give up. We got in the car and eventually found a post office in Old City, where we sat on the floor and filled out the labels. People began to expect their cookie treats every year.

This year I will fill my time with cookie making, using the old kitchen table, to honor both my girls.

When I go into my file cabinet, I find our old recipes and discover Suzanne's handwritten calculations to double, triple, and quadruple them. Also, in her writing are her shopping lists. Every word is precious to me: *8 cups of flour. 2 cups of chocolate chips.* I'm not alone because Suzanne is still helping me with cookie day.

CHAPTER 54

Danger Zone

"We are in the danger zone," Rachel Maddow says as I am getting ready to bake. "We are at the point where almost 3000 people a day are dying and that's going to exponentially increase over these next couple of months." I do the math and it scares me. That's two people a minute! Hospitals are overrun. I tell my Mom it's time for her to stay home and receive food orders. She doesn't like that, but who does? She reluctantly, agrees.

We are in the danger zone and I am having more frequent Afib episodes. We do what we can do. We are in the danger zone and I'm baking cookies. Whatever works.

Cookie making is a good idea and ultimately is successful, but has a rough start. My electric mixer breaks while I am in the middle of preparing the gingerbread dough. I run to Kitchen Kapers, an everything store for kitchens, and they don't have them. "Mixers are hard to come by, these days," a salesperson tells me. Damn pandemic!

Where to next? Macy's! It is only about a 10-minute walk to the store, but on the way, I get a giant panic attack. *What if Macy's doesn't have them and I can't make the cookies in time? And I've bought all these ingredients!* I began to feel faint, and weak, like I could pass out. I lean against a building to rest, hoping my heart rate slows. When I take the escalator up to the 3rd floor of Macy's, everything has been re-arranged. Furniture has replaced the housewares. Completely dazed and confused, I sit on a nearby sofa to reassure myself that I'm not having a bad dream. At that moment I get a text from an old lover. This note becomes a distraction and takes my mind off my confusion.

"Do you need help?" I hear a voice and look up to see a salesperson standing over me. I'm sure I need a lot of help. All kinds of help. But I say, "Do you have electric mixers?" She shows me where the new housewares department is and points to the hand mixers nearly arranged on a shelf. No shortages in Macy's, not at all. Once I have my hands around the Black and Decker mixer box, I begin to feel more grounded. And by the time I am on the bus, checking my phone, the whole panic attack is over.

Time to get back to acupuncture—it seems I am still "elevated."

With my shiny new mixer center stage, I get back to the gingerbread. Mandel bread and chocolate chips will be next. Tomorrow it's Russian tea cakes and peanut butter Kiss cookies. If I have the energy, lime coolers and maybe, oatmeal. Definitely the lime coolers. Suzanne loved the lime green colored frosting. The old kitchen table grows crowded with cookies.

Cookie making helps to fill the space of time. I do yoga in the morning and write during a coffee break. I nibble on a broken piece of tea cake and the hard end of the mandel bread with a chocolate chip in the last bite — a little surprise. My apartment smells like a bakery. Even my bath towels smell like baked cookies. I am grateful for my sense of smell, for so many are losing it to Covid. I've heard that Covid may interfere with a man's erection. Don't know if it's true, but maybe it will inspire our male politicians to get the vaccine out there more quickly.

The race to create a vaccine makes its way into my dreams.

The dream…

There's a special fish somewhere that is helping to discover the vaccine. I have my own tank of fish and I am lucky because my Kamala fish had already mated with the special fish before I got her and now she can mate with my regular guppies. The special fish had a gene that transferred when it mated with the Kamala fish and now I have her offspring in my tank.

The theory was that if the special fish came into my tank and mated with the offspring of the Kamala fish, that we would have a vaccine. We were thinking about how to transport the six-inch-long special fish to my tank, to mate with my tiny guppies, but when I go home, just one fish remains flopping around in my sink and all the water has gone down the drain. I try to fill up the sink with water, but the stopper isn't working because it isn't a stopper at all — only a drain.

A couple days later the FDA approves a real vaccine, and in a week emergency and hospital workers will get the first doses. It will take months for everyone else to get vaccinated. This feels hopeful.

I've gotten out the 16 tins of cookies, but the mail is slow. Excruciatingly slow. And there's no guarantee that folks will get their cookies before Christmas. I can't do a damn thing about it, just as I can't make the rollout of the vaccine any faster than it is, although it looks like the Kamala fish came through!

I also can't stop the undercurrent of stress running throughout the country as the election counts have finally ended. For the first time in our country's history, we're not sure if there will be a peaceful transition of power as there is talk of violence on Jan. 6th, the day the election is to be certified. This can't be our country. The layers pile on.

And it's scary.

I take a week-long watercolor class and sign up for a figure drawing/painting class for January. Artwork relaxes and heals me. I also agree to volunteer as an online "Reading Partner" twice a week until May. My eight-year-old student "loves to read about butterflies," but needs help. I'm hoping that I can do something positive for him. Anxiety starts to creep in. *What if I mess up the technology? What if my student doesn't like me?* They put an "aide" in our breakout room because I need a lot of tech help. My new young friend seems shy as he slumps down in his chair with a hoodie pulled over his head. I attempt to establish a relationship by asking about his interest in butterflies. We take turns reading and I can see his struggles. As we continue, he starts to "play" with me by turning his camera and mic on and off. I have to keep calling for him. And it's frustrating. I feel myself starting to panic—I've lost control.

"Your anxiety is lying to you," I read on Twitter that morning. My anxiety might be lying, but it's not logical. Try reasoning with a panic attack. *Maybe I have set my expectations too high. Maybe my inability to "save" Suzanne, makes my desire stronger to help or save others. Maybe that's crazy. I am not that powerful.*

During our session there are more interruptions—a barking dog and a noisy family member. My student opens up a bit more when I ask him about the football "sticker" he has chosen for his account. Philadelphians are crazy about football! When the session is over, I am so relieved, but my body reacts and I get full-blown Afib. It's frustrating, but I don't give up. *Things can only get better,* I tell myself. This poor kid— he's got Zoom school and then Zoom extra reading. We do what we can do. I fix myself a bowl of split pea soup with smoked turkey neck and relax with Netflix. Smoked turkey saves this day.

I go to sleep with Afib but wake up feeling fine. Feeling normal instead of Afibby is such a contrast. *What is wrong with me? Sometimes I feel so good and then Wham! Anxiety pops in.*

I am dreaming about turkey breast. Platters and platters of sliced turkey breast at a big catered affair, but I'm not hungry.

This time I know exactly why I am having this dream. Mom's online food orders have become an ordeal. I have access to the shopper, so I leave specific notes about mom's choices. She is picky about her food, and she has dietary restrictions: low salt and no sugar.

One time, when I am on my way to the rental office to settle a bill, Demetrius, Mom's "shopper of the day", texts me obsessively with questions about every single food item. I tell him I had already written some instructions about the items—including the low-sodium deli turkey breast. He starts to argue with me saying he didn't have the instructions. We are both a little *elevated.* Then silence. Soon I get a message saying the shopper "couldn't complete the order." I imagine him abandoning the shopping cart in the aisle— maybe even running out of the store screaming and quitting his job because of Mom's turkey breast selection. Who knows? This is so frustrating. Soon a new shopper, Yin Feng, takes over. He has some common sense, manners, and grace. The only question he has is about the turkey breast. Yin Feng saves the day and Mom gets her perfectly completed order on time.

Who knew turkey would play such a leading role in my pandemic stories? Necks and now breasts!

I continue walking on Spruce Street to the rental office. Because of our unreliable mail service, the December rent check hadn't arrived. After waiting a couple of weeks, I had decided to hand deliver a new one. I present the current rent check along with another one for January. What a great idea! Now, I won't have the mail to worry about. But no. Without consulting me, they cash the January check early and it bounces. "We don't hold checks," they tell me. And they charge me a $15 fee for the bounced check—and act like I should be grateful because they usually charge $50. The bank understands the challenges of the pandemic and waives its fee. The bank has become my hero.

All this drama makes me angry. Why aren't people competent? The rental company, the shopper Demetrius, and people who won't wear masks. I'm angry with the scary armed people showing up at state capitols to try to overthrow the election. I'm angry and I'm afraid. And now a new virus variant has shown up in a few states. There is so much uncertainty about what's coming in the new year, it's hard to be optimistic.

CHAPTER 55

Insurrection

Jan. 6, 2021

I am sitting in the salon surrounded by panes of plexiglass. As my hair dye seeps in, I decide to check my phone. It's around 1:30 and at the Capitol in DC violent, aggressive protesters, spurred on by the outgoing president and other politicians, are storming the building. When I get home I become transfixed to the television watching the horror before me. Rioters calling to hang Vice President Pence. The construction of a gallows. This feels so surreal, so un-American. And it takes too long for the National Guard to be called, as if the outgoing president, doesn't care or worse-supports the destruction. An insurrection! Lawmakers and staff have to hide, wear gas masks, and run for their lives. People die and dozens of Capitol Police are injured. I am numb. This doesn't happen here. But it does.

Democracy prevails this time. Our elected officials stay until the early morning hours to certify the election.

Days later, I watch video clips on TV and social media. I can see how the whole thing could have ended even worse, if not for one lone police officer who diverted the mob from the senate chambers.

Jan. 20th, Inauguration Day, can't come fast enough.

I go outside for a walk. On Chestnut Street a long line waits outside to get into Sephora. Apparently after a violent attempted coup, skin care and makeup are still required.

I don't cry until I see a Twitter post that I've seen before—a flash mob performing Beethoven's "Ode to Joy." A solitary cello plays in a European square. Gradually it builds to include a full orchestra and chorus. Because it has been almost a year of pandemic restrictions, we are weary. This post shows civility, beauty, and the freedom of people gathering to make beautiful music, unlike the angry destructive mob in support of a would-be dictator. The rioters urinated on desks; spread their feces on the walls of the People's House; and crushed officers in doorways. The contrast hits me hard. *How can this be my country? This can't be.* I weep.

When I dry my tears, I notice the afternoon sun pouring through the windows. It is almost a year since returning from Morocco when I hobbled up my apartment steps, becoming Rapunzel in the castle, going down only for physical therapy appointments. Now, I am able to walk normally. And dance! I have lived through the loss of two children, 9/11, and now this. The human spirit is strong and soon we will have a human president. Birds are singing, even in January. They know that spring is not so far away.

We all hold our breath on Inauguration Day, but precautions are taken in case any rabble-rousers attempt more violence. The Secret Service has deemed it a "safe event."

Also "safe" was the memorial held the night before for those who have died from Covid. *It's about time*, I think, *that we acknowledge the victims*. It has been so chaotic, there hasn't been time to mourn. The new administration is so human. I had forgotten what human was. I let the tears flow. Sweet release.

Everything goes perfectly. Class and decency are back in the White House. Rachel Maddow says that they have used every available firework in DC, so if you are looking for any, you won't find them. I feel myself exhale. For now.

The former president crawls back into the floor boards of his broken soul and awaits the next lawsuit and/or trial. I don't care. Do you?

CHAPTER 56

More Adjustments Needed

At the end of the month, I get a call from my mother. She's fallen again, almost a year after her first fall, but she had managed to get up and is "fine." I want her to go to the hospital, but she doesn't want to go. After a couple of days, she decides it's time and ends up in the emergency room, where they check her out and agree that she's "fine" but her bruises will hurt for a while.

Another week passes and she doesn't feel great. It is the dead of winter and we are having a snowstorm. Guilt shows up again. *I should be doing more to help her.* I start to *re-think* Mom being in NY and me in PA. Not being able to easily check in on her is not great. I need eyes on her to know how she really is. She hates to bother me, so I'm never sure if she is telling me the truth. *I was away from Suzanne when she died. Will the same happen with my Mom?* I have to do the best for her, so I bring up the idea of assisted living. She doesn't respond, but I've planted the seed.

My friend Lynn, who got me into the drum group, has her mom Elsie in the Watermark, a senior facility, right here in Philly. Lynn and I grew up as neighbors on Long Island and our moms played mahjong once a week for years. It was a surprise when I ran into her some years ago at one of my library dance programs. We had kept in touch since then. One day in February Lynne posts on Facebook the cutest photo of 95-year-old Elsie, sitting inside a big frame that says, "I've been vaccinated." The vaccines have made their way quickly into senior facilities and nursing homes which were hit hard by Covid. *Wouldn't it be nice if Mom were there?. She'd already be vaccinated.* Lynn tells me I can get Mom an apartment for a reasonable price in independent living which includes some meals. It sounds like the perfect thing. She could be independent with a little extra care.

A dream…

I am swimming with Suzanne and my mom to an island where we are welcomed by exotic Asian people with food and flowers. I don't know what language to speak so I am silent.

Is this "island" the Watermark? Looks like Suzanne will be with us all the way. Hello, Sweetness.

While we wish for winter to end, we also wait to receive our vaccines. I busy myself with art classes. The teacher of the figure class is outstanding. He gets me out of my comfort zone and stimulates my creativity. His advice, "Do less with more," makes me think he is a Zen master. I am so excited by this teacher; he is just what I need at this time. My heart starts to beat fast and my head explodes from his wisdom. "Make a mess. Get lost. Find your way out." He is talking about art, but it is good advice for life. Advice I need to hear right now.

So I do, I get lost in the work. I forget to eat. I am all into the creativity. I fill up the space with art, yoga, and more dance classes. There are more weepy acupuncture sessions. Time goes by.

My mother tells me that my cousin Rozzy shows up in her dream. She takes my Mom to visit my dad's parents, who kiss. "It was so real," she said. "That's because it was a visit," I tell her.

Since her fall, she's had difficulty walking and has begun using an old walker that Suzanne had tucked away in her closet "for the future." I'm wondering why she's not feeling better. She doesn't want help, but she complains about everything. What do you do when you think someone is not taking care of themselves, but they refuse help? "You witness it," Cate says. She also suggests I call mom's social worker, so I do.

I think about Suzanne and all the help she had over the years: psychiatric facilities, drug rehabs, AA, therapy, Family School, halfway house, detox, more therapy, more AA, Kripalu, breathwork, and yoga. When she relapsed, I had to witness the downfall. And it wasn't pretty.

There's no way in hell, I'm not going to do everything I can for my mom!

CHAPTER 57

Off the Hook

What if I just take myself off the hook for Suzanne's suicide?

I write these words one morning. The fires of brain pain have worn me down. I admit, I'm tired of the fight. What if I stop thinking of all the ways I could have saved her and of all the mistakes I made? I've seen her struggles in the journals. What if I look only at Suzanne's essence, her purity when she wasn't affected by substances? How about I start from there?

These questions enter my mind while I read. Lately, words and ideas, seem to have taken hold with fresher, deeper meanings, and I hear new wisdom.

A book I'm reading, *The Soul's Plan, says we* choose our life's experiences before we take birth, some souls "sacrificing" for the growth of other souls. If that is true, I am to thank my children for allowing me to experience pain, discomfort, and guilt, so my soul can learn what? Forgiveness? Self-forgiveness? I have forgiven so many people in my life, why not myself?

I'm also reading about Zen Buddhist monk Ikkyu, who wanted his life to be different for so many years. But then, one day when he hears a crow's call, he realizes the Now. Just like that. In a moment. If I stay with continuous guilt, I am in the past. Where is the Now? If I am anxious, I am fearful of the future. Muddling in the guilt keeps me in the past. What is my crow's call?

Maybe it is my writing.

Every day I read from *The Pocket Pema Chodron*, but lately, the words have more power. It's like I am hearing them for the first time. Pema talks about living life with curiosity, as an "experiment." What if I experiment with this?

What if I just take myself off the hook for Suzanne's suicide?

And see what that feels like.

It's worth a try.

✳ ✳ ✳

I wake up the next morning full of creative ideas. I'm thinking of a children's book about my girls, which I could illustrate. Maybe all my artwork has prepared me for that. Children's books, young adult books, and adult books—I can do them all. The prospect of doing my own artwork is thrilling. Now that I am experimenting with taking myself off the hook, I am determined not to let the circumstances of Suzanne's death prevent me from honoring her life.

It's just another opportunity to practice letting go. I can hear Suzanne's voice in my head. When I let go of pain and guilt, I don't have to let go of Suzanne. Releasing guilt does not mean I'll forget my daughter. My experience with Lisa tells me that it will never happen. Reminders are everywhere. And ultimately, the sweeter ones last. From the space where the guilt was, fresh memories will emerge. In letting go, I open up the channels to work *with* my kids and not *against* them.

There is something in these words which feels good and solid and real and authentic. I trust my gut, and believe them to be truth.

CHAPTER 58

Taking Charge

Five weeks after Mom's fall, she wakes up and can't put any pressure on her foot. Instead of calling me, she calls Brenda, my aunt's aide, and she comes right over. Brenda calls me and we decide that she needs to go back to the hospital. This time they find a fracture in her right hip and surgery is necessary. Don't ask me why they didn't see this the first time. I feel relieved that we know what's going on. Hopefully, she will get PT and OT afterwards and she will have a speedy recovery like she did after last year's surgery.

Brenda says Mom's apartment is filthy, and volunteers to do some cleaning. It looks like leaving Mom to her own care has its ugly consequences. And an unpleasant reality is seeping in.

Now I feel really bad. This distance between us is not sustainable. I realize that I can't trust Mom's judgment. Steps must be taken now to make some changes. First surgery, then rehab. Then we will talk about care for her and Power of Attorney. I wish she would consider coming to Philly.

I think about 2015, when Suzanne stayed with me before she moved to Dallas. I encouraged her to go when she was indecisive, but told her she could always make another choice. She had come home before, from Nashville, with my car and credit card. I think about how her distance from me prevented me from seeing clearly what was going on in her life. That can't happen with my Mom.

***

After a successful operation with no pain, Mom is so much better. My heart is singing. Three days later she's in rehab. We are still in the "no visitors" time of the pandemic, but that is supposed to change soon now that vaccines are available. She's already walking with the walker. It's a miracle!

My online writing class starts this week and I am still taking the art class. I have plenty of outlets for distraction, and can also take care of what needs to be done for Mom. Right now, she's in good hands.

Another dream…

My kids are little and I am getting them dressed for a library program. Suz and I are having a big laugh—we have turned ourselves upside down and think we look like upside-down penguins.

Hearing her laugh as a child is the sweetest sound. She's letting me know she's close.

Although I have confidence in Mom's rehab, I can't help feeling guilty that I am not able to do more. It's clear that releasing guilt for Suzanne is giving me space to fully grasp my role in Mom's care. First things first. As if I need reassurance that Mom is not alone, there are more dreams…

I am visiting Suzanne in rehab at the hospital and I get to hug and kiss her. She looks good, filled out a little and fresh without makeup. My mom and my grandmother are there too. There's a classical music concert for "family day." I was late because I had to see the doctor, myself, and I'm still waiting for a test result.

The message is clear. Mom's got Suzanne and her mother Sophie, and they want me to take care of myself too. And the hugging! Hugging is off limits with Covid. My dream world is rich with life.

As I impatiently wait to get vaccinated, I think about all the things I could be doing at Mom's place to get it ready for her return. I put in my information online several times and come up "not eligible," and I'm frustrated. So much waiting. It is the second week of March and violet crocuses are making their appearance.. The weather is warm enough for me to remove my leather jacket as I stroll through the neighborhood. Soon I will get vaccinated. Soon there will be hugs again. Have I forgotten them? There is always change. Change is the only constant.

I finally speak to Mom's physical therapist who says the goal for her is to walk confidently with a walker when she goes home. "No cane?" I ask. Mom is hoping to get back to the cane. With this injury and her poor balance, that is no longer an option. More change.

March 15th is my vaccine day! The requirements now include over 65 and I'm excited to qualify as a senior. After a frigid 25-minute walk to the Convention Center, I have to wait on a massive line that curves around the block but moves quickly.

This is my first time at a FEMA site, which is a good thing because that means I haven't been in a disaster. I'm impressed by the efficiency and compassion of the National Guard seamlessly running the operation. As I sit and receive the shot, I well up. Finally, after all this waiting, there will be more freedom and less worry. I'm proud my country has this federal program to handle the Covid disaster—America at its best. Last stop in the process, I make an appointment for the 2nd dose. In two weeks I'll finally be covered and can visit Mom.

A week later Mom gets her 1st vaccine in rehab. She will have to go back there for her 2nd dose. We are on our way to protection, as things begin to open up. First, museums — bars will be next. The world is coming back to life! Hallelujah. Meanwhile, as mom is resting in rehab, she enjoys reading in her chair and having meals brought to her. Again I bring up the subject of coming to the Watermark in

Philly. "Life will be easier,' I tell her, "and I will be within walking distance." I remind her that her old friend Elsie is there. She responds, "I'm not going to say no." *Wait, what? Do I sense a shift? An opening?*

The truth is Suzanne always talked about bringing Grandma to Philly. As a nurse, she had seen so many situations where people had to scramble to make arrangements for their aging parents. She thought that a preemptive move would be wise. But in the years when Suzanne lived here, my mom wasn't ready. Driving and shopping and having lunch with her sister, sometimes going to the casinos together, she had a rich and full life in Queens. But now, things have changed. She will be using a walker. And managing that with her staircase will be impossible.

I feel like Suzanne is beside me, with one hand on my back, guiding me through this process. And she is smiling. She may finally get her wish.

I'm fine, I hear her whisper in my ear. *We have work to do!*

I make an appointment to see the facility.

PART IV
Beyond

CHAPTER 59

Time for a Move

Sitting in the Watermark's lobby, a Frank Sinatra tune in the background, I gaze out at the wall of windows. Daylight fills the room. I decide to text Lynn while waiting for my guided tour and it turns out that she and her brother Steve are visiting their mom today. I couldn't have planned this. It feels auspicious.

I fall in love with the facility and can't find anything wrong. I had envisioned a nursing home with frail people, but this feels more like a fancy hotel with vibrant seniors living their lives. It far exceeds my expectations. Mom can have a one-bedroom apartment, almost exactly like the one in Queens, and she can bring most of her furniture to keep it as familiar as possible.

Before I leave, I go up to Elsie's apartment to see the family. She is a few years older than Mom and has an aide. Although I was 24 when my mom moved out of our old neighborhood, Elsie remembers me as a child. "Little Roberta," she calls me and says she sees me as a tough little tomboy running all over the neighborhood and playing sports with the boys. Lynn and Steve are okay with me hugging her as she is fully vaccinated and I have one dose, so Elsie kisses me on top of my mask along with the hugs. She doesn't want to let go. She doesn't remember that she had attended Suzanne's memorial four years prior.

When Mom hears how excited I am about the place, she goes all in. She trusts me to make the right decisions. My goal is to move her there sooner rather than later.

There will be a tearful and affectionate reunion three months later when Elsie and Mom first see each other in the dining room.

It takes more than a minute to get Mom there. There is so much to do: clean out the attic; get rid of a lifetime of stuff; hire packers and movers; and sell her place. The Philly apartment needs a new bed, recliner, and small dining table. It's all on me. How will it ever get done?

Anxiety returns when I think of all the tasks, but I feel like I have the support of Suzanne and others who have passed. *You're not doing this alone,* my cousin Roz had written in one of her last texts before Covid took her. I feel her close.

Everything moves quicker and easier than expected. My cousin Stan recommends a lawyer friend Susan, and a realtor friend Harold, who had lived across the street from Mom for years. Mom remembers Harold and loves him. So we are ready to make this happen after she returns home from rehab.

It is the second week in April and I've taken Amtrak to Mom's for a few days to get the place ready for her return. It's been a year since I've made this trip. The train rolls into Manhattan's shiny new Moynahan Train Hall which used to be the post office on 8th Avenue. It's gorgeous and modern. Soooo much nicer than the dingy old Penn Station. I see this as a good omen. Fresh starts all around.

When I get to Mom's place, there are some challenges. I run into a big fat leak in her bathroom. When maintenance attempts to fix the original 50-year-old sink, the parts crumble—they have to replace it. Then her car won't start. Maintenance again to the rescue with a jump. But now I'm worried the car will stall again. I go to a couple of markets to fill mom's fridge with her favorites and cook a bunch of chicken so she'll have some meals. The frying chicken sets off the smoke alarm, which eventually stops after I open all the windows. It's too much stress and I get Afib. Adrenaline keeps me going with little sleep because there's lots more to do.

It's as if the apartment is telling us it's time to go. My decision to move Mom to Philly is confirmed.

After settling mom home from rehab, I begin the journey home. First the Long Island Railroad to Manhattan–then the slow and pokey New Jersey Transit to Trenton, where I wait 50 minutes for the SEPTA train to Philly. Eventually I will get home. Reading and doing crosswords pass the time. I wonder how the hell I did this kind of commuting regularly for 10 years when I was a face painter? I am so done with it. Amtrak is the only way to do this. Mom can't move to Philly fast enough.

In the meantime, I have some new mantras: *Everything is temporary. Everything will get done.* And it is. And it will. Maybe with a glitch or two, but all will get done.

I schedule Mom's PT and OT visits. There are endless doctor's appointments. These will become what I refer to as the "goodbye doctor tour," where Mom gets to say farewell to all the medical professionals she's visited for years.

Back home, I get some support from my Mom's (who have lost children) Group, now online because of the pandemic. They let me vent about the move. This is the first time I feel as if the group is helping me. I feel heard and validated for what I am doing. I need this. I share with them about making the decision to "take myself off the hook" for Suzanne. *Good thing I did. I need the energy for Mom.* Weekly acupuncture helps with the stress as I am getting more Afib episodes.

A few days after Harold puts Mom's place on the market, there are already a couple of offers. Wow, that's fast! This move has suddenly become very real. Harold figures 3–4 months for the whole process. I begin to view this project like one of the shows I worked on in the schools. Planning had to be organized and efficient, so that everything got done by showtime. Moving day is showtime. I can do this!

CHAPTER 60

Surprise Gifts

As moving responsibilities expand, the Natalie Goldberg writing class comes to an end. Something (or someone—Suzanne??) tells me to post on the course's Facebook page to see if any Philly peeps might want to continue writing practice. In the back of my mind, I know I'm pretty booked up for the next few months with the move, but I figure this could be something ongoing. Four serious responses become a new bi-weekly writing group. The same post also connects me with an old Sayville friend, Eleanor. She says that her whole body went into chills when she realized it was me after over 20 years! We have a great phone conversation—like no time has passed, and agree to get together via Zoom or Facetime every couple of weeks.

Offers on mom's place, a new writing group, and a re-kindled friendship—all on the same day! The Universe is wasting no time with manifesting my intentions. By releasing guilt, there is so much energetic space for the new. Why do I feel like Suzanne (and Lisa) are loving this so much? Maybe because they are.

A dream…

I am making pancakes with the girls. (When Lisa was little she called them "pakes.") *There's a big bowl of butter on the table. Suzanne wants French toast, so I make hers separately.*

Everything is better with butter. I don't know who said that, but it's definitely true. The sweetness of this dream matches my feelings of contentment. Everything seems to be flowing with ease.

It doesn't take long for us to settle on a buyer. A NYC fireman makes the best offer. Mom likes him because when he comes in to see her apartment, he pokes his head in the bedroom to say hello to her. Manners go a long way, plus the extra cash. Within a week contracts are signed. Everyone wants to make this happen quickly, especially me, since I am doing all the commuting. I know Suzanne is helping.

One day when I'm there, Mom's foot is swollen and her surgeon recommends compression stockings. We struggle to get them on and off. We pull and push, inch by inch. We try to squeeze her flesh into the fabric. It's hard work and I begin to sweat. In the end, we laugh about it and make it a big joke, but on the inside I'm concerned. This would be a great time to have Nurse Suzanne by my side. *Should I persist? I'm not trained in this. What if we are doing it wrong?* I don't. I give up. I put a cold compress on her foot and arrange some pillows so she can raise it when she sleeps. I don't know if any of this is helping or hurting.

When I go home, I worry about it all night. It is too much. In the morning, I'm still anxious. I am back to thinking that I am killing her. "I thought you would wake up dead," I tell her. She finds this hilarious, so I know she's alive. "I'm fine," she tells me and I burst into sobs of relief. This is the most involved I have ever been in my mom's ailments. All I have to do is trust that Nurse Suzanne is guiding me to do the right thing.

For a peaceful diversion, I have arranged a llama walk for my Mom's support group. We drive to real farmland in the middle of New Jersey It's important to note that we are not riding them, so no falls. We will walk with them to have a peaceful experience in nature. When we are introduced to the llamas, a big white fluffy one, Eduardo, "hugs" me. Technically, it's not a hug, but a lean into, and I could instantly feel the healing. Even after a few minutes of greeting time, we can see their personalities emerge. I get assigned to Clemente, a black and white shaggy boy. We bring up the rear and guide each other along the wooded path. With the sun shining on a perfect cloudless day, every muscle in my body relaxes and I am at peace. Suzanne loves this too. I'm sure of it.

In the calmness of the day, I forget all about Mom for a little bit. Whew!

***

Dammit! Another mom fall, this time when I'm there. I hear a thud. "Roberta!" she screams my name. I rush into her room and see her crumpled on the floor. I surmise that she had leaned on her lightweight walker as she got out of bed and fell forward, head first into her wooden closet, then bounced and fell to the floor. Her emergency button goes off and the EMT's show up within minutes. "Put on some clothes," she yells at me, as I am trying to see if she's okay. Clearly, she is fine. They bring her to the hospital where tests and scans show everything is normal. The giant bruise on her face, seems to grow daily and is the only reminder of this scare. Time to upgrade the walker to something more sturdy!

I'm with Mom as she says goodbye to her favorite—Dr. Mandel, as we near the end of her "farewell to doctors" tour. It's hard to see her with a bruised purple face. It's also hard to see Mom saying goodbye to her doctor friends, but then I think it is necessary. It is a closure ceremony, making the transition easier and complete.

Mom's hearing aid battery dies on our last "farewell" visit, so she doesn't get to hear all the sweet things her diabetes doctor tells her. Before we leave, he says privately to me,"You're doing all the right things," which makes me feel validated for my efforts. So maybe I'm not killing my Mom? I start to well up. He gets it. He has Suzanne's compassion.

CHAPTER 61

Showtime

Suzanne finally gets her wish. July 7th, 2021, is Move Mom to Philly Day. *Grandma's coming to Philly!!* Paperwork is being completed and deposits made. She'll stay in the guest suite at the Watermark, a furnished apartment, while I go back to Queens and deal with packers and movers. A week later, she will move into apartment # 1010. During that week, new furniture will be delivered. After that, all I'll have left is the closing on her apartment and returning the leased car. It's almost showtime.

A billboard of a giant Geico gecko greets us in Philly as Mom and I roll into the city. Hello Suzanne!

Everything moves smoothly. The new furniture arrives on schedule and mom settles into the guest suite. She is very impressed with the place and its friendly staff. The flow continues in Queens as cleaning and moving the remaining furniture is easy.

When I follow the movers back to Phllly we unpack a few boxes. Then, I take off for some me time—a live show at the City Winery. At my first live music in over a year, a small masked and vaccinated crowd has ventured out to this classy venue to see Wynonna. Congratulations to me, with two glasses of Prosecco and a kale caesar salad with shrimp. I did it. I really did it. There are more boxes, the car, and the closing to deal with, but Mom is in and I'm finished with her Queens place. This is big. I'm relieved and excited for Mom to begin her next adventure in Philly.

I'm so glad that I celebrated, but I am burning the candle at both ends. The next day I feel like I'm coming down with something—a messed up stomach and maybe a bladder infection. I've been missing my yoga, dance, and home downtime. I'm depleted and exhausted. We manage to get through a few boxes and I pick up groceries for Mom. It's hot and humid as I carry the packages from Whole Foods. On my bus ride home, I look down and notice that I'm wearing two different colored sandals—one beige and one black (I have two pairs same style). How did that happen? Overworked? Distracted mind? Mom doesn't notice. Maybe other people do. No one says anything. Lordy! I'm losing it!

After I bring back the car, one last trip to Queens remains. I can taste my life coming back to me. I need to detox from NYC commuting. It's coming.

After the closing, I celebrate with a vanilla ice cream with chocolate sprinkles while I wait for the train in Great Neck. I think about the experience—how nice the fireman couple was. They gave us a box of chocolates (a Korean custom). I note that both Harold's partner and the buyer's lawyer are named Lisa. My lawyer is Susan. That's close enough for me. Lisa's and Suzanne's seal of approval!

CHAPTER 62

Crash and Revival

A few days later, I feel myself begin to crash. My whole upper body aches and I feel like I'm going to cry. I've been on a mission, putting one foot in front of the other and accomplishing each next task. Running on adrenalin and sheer will, all is complete. And similar to after the performance of a school show, there is a let-down. I feel it now. Coming off the adrenalin, I weep. I let myself sob it out until I'm finished.

To give myself something to look forward to, I have planned a few days of writing at Pendle Hill, a Quaker retreat center about 30 minutes outside the city. Suzanne loved the Quakers. She would always tell me that. *Wasn't Philadelphia founded by them?*

After my emotional release, I begin to clean my place from top to bottom and get rid of clutter. I'm hosting our new writing group for the first time and it feels good to tidy up and get rid of what I don't need. I begin to gather up my writing practice notebooks for the retreat. It has been three years since my last visit to Pendle HIll, in 2018 when I was working on my first book. Having a nice long stretch of uninterrupted writing is a luxury I cherish.

Pendle HIll is just what the doctor ordered. A lush peaceful place with giant ancient trees and nothing to do but walk around the grounds and trails. It's refreshing and a sharp contrast from city sounds and smells. The hot and humid weather keeps me in my air-conditioned room where I write and write and write. I come out only for meals.

After lunch, I sit outside and read a little of Richard A. Heckler's *Waking up Alive—The Descent, The Suicide Attempt and the The Return to Life.* It is the only book I've found that interviews people who attempted suicide and lived. He says that "Suicide attempters say they were certain that no one could possibly enter their worlds ...with compassion, and comprehend the depth of their suffering." They also thought no one would want to. Some of them have no idea how they ever got to the point of ending their lives. It starts with a gradual withdrawal, until they are just going through motions. Then there is the "trance," when they are no longer able to recognize that support exists—they believe they have no other choice. I got to understand that myself when I experienced that incident in the cafe—I had been isolating and keeping everything in. So did Suzanne.

On my last full day, I decide to take my lunch to the outdoor patio. Two workmen sit at the table next to mine. "How did you end up in Philly?" they ask me. "My daughter used to live here," I respond. A few moments of silence. The younger workman continues.

"Does she live here now?"

"No." More silence.

"Was her name Suzanne?"

What??? This guy knew Suzanne?

He recognized me from her "beautiful" memorial. I can't believe this! There are about 20 people on the Pendle Hill campus and I end up sitting next to him! He also helped Suzanne move from Chestnut Street to Market Street, and was her first AA sponser when she moved to Philly after the Family School. He sponsered her boyfriend, too. "They were wild, almost feral," he tells me with a smile. He knew her well. "There are countless people whose lives she altered by her amazing recovery," he adds. "She sponsered many and ran meetings." I am speechless! What are the chances?

I have come here to write about Suzanne and me, and she's here. She's here in this man's memory. She lives on in the countless people she helped in AA, as a nurse, and just being her sparkling self.

That night I have a dream…

I am in a deli and the workers are super sad because someone in their family has died. Their faces are the long and ashen faces of grief. I go to the young woman who has come out from behind the counter and hug her. Her body falls into mine and we breathe together. I whisper to her, "I understand grief." "Tell me about it," she says. And I tell.

"It comes in waves. Everyone grieves differently, so don't judge. Take one day at a time, sometimes one hour at a time. It doesn't go away, but changes."

Then I break from the hug and ask the young man behind the counter if he wants to make me a sandwich. He nods. I ask for a turkey and swiss on a roll with mustard, lettuce, and tomatoes. And I wake up.

My dream makes me think of a couple of Zen sayings:

Afer enlightenment, the laundry.

Before enlightenment chop wood, carry water. After enlightenment, chop wood carry water.

In the dream I talk about grief. I share what has taken me years to understand. Then I ask for a sandwich (turkey!!) it seems so simple, but reality is more complicated. Grief takes as long as it takes.

✳ ✳ ✳

When I get home, something has shifted. I begin to think about travelling to Iceland, which has always been on my bucket list. I'm fascinated by this wild, unspoiled place with its volcanoes, waterfalls, and areas that look like moonscapes. And Reykjavik, its capital, is full of charm and creativity.

Maybe I can see the Northern Lights. And why not? It takes about a day and half after the thought bubble to search the internet, purchase a guide book, check reviews, and book the trip. Easiest booking I've ever done. It feels right.

Some of my friends think that I've gone crazy when I tell them I am planning a trip to Iceland for mid-December. I will be there for the Winter Solstice, the shortest day of the year. They try to show support, but I can see that their faces are twisted and contorted as they are trying to figure out what has happened to their friend Roberta who wants to go to a frigid dark wilderness in winter. I know that there's way more than that. The more I research, the more excited I become. My friends who have been there understand.

CHAPTER 63

Suzanne Shows Up

At this week's writing group, the topic is "August" and all I can write about is Suzanne.

Soon it will be four years since Suzanne's passing and I have come a long way in the processing, the acceptance, in the releasing of guilt. The memories have not always been pleasant, but sweeter ones are shining through. I'll never know if any of the should, could, or would haves might have made any difference. And I am content to live with uncertainty. Her state of mind at the end was altered and she was not who she was in her heart and soul. I know that now. Now I just miss her...

The group is silent as I read and cry. Paula leaves and comes back with a box of tissues. Afterward, Eleanor reveals that she lost a brother to suicide. Marianne tells me that she's changed the way she deals with her daughters after hearing my story. We are all here to share stories, to hold space for others in reverent silence. In stillness and attention, we honor each others' hearts—heavy or light, broken or bursting.

***

On Suzanne's anniversary I am obsessed with finding a 2008 YouTube video of her and her boyfriend at the XPN music festival. I hadn't seen it in years and I remember how sweet it was.

Dear Suzanne,

When I dug up the YouTube video of you and Paulie at the XPN festival, I saw how beautiful and radiant you were. I feel like that's how I want to remember you — your true soul shining through.

2008. The year brings memories — exciting wonderful times we shared when I moved to Phily. How sweet it was to live nearby. I think how our relationship blossomed. And here's Suzanne in the video looking like a Disney princess, reminding me of the magic.

* * *

A week later I step into Garland of Letters a New Age bookstore on South Street. Nina Simone's rich earthy version of "Suzanne" plays in the background. *Hello, Sweetness.*

It was 20 years ago when my ex-husband and I stopped here and bought the Truth stone. I am overcome with emotion and have to fight back tears. "You want to travel with her…she's touched your perfect body with her mind." Nina Simone is singing this directly to me. Two books fall into my hands, *How to Live When a Loved One Dies,* by

Thich Nhat Hanh and *Zen and the Art of Writing,* by Ray Bradbury. They become mine. Thanks Suzanne!

Earlier I had taken a big walk assessing damage done by heavy rains the night before that caused the Schuylkill River to overflow and the neighborhood to lose power. Waters of 8–10 feet covered the river trail and the train tracks. I'm so glad my roof is fixed. The floods made it to the dog park and through the River Park, all the way up to 25th Street.

On my walk down South Street, I think about another time before Suzanne moved to Dallas, when she and I wandered around the neighborhood "assessing" damage after a hurricane. Back then, there were just a few puddles on the river trail. It became a little joke between us because after all the TV warnings, nothing really happened in Philly. "Let's go assess," we'd say after a storm, meeting each other's eyes and laughing.

✳ ✳ ✳

"I want to speak to Roberta."

I'm glued to the computer screen at a Zoom group medium event when I hear these words.

For 20 bucks or so, you can be in a live Zoom audience and if you are lucky a medium (some of them very well known) may connect you briefly with your loved ones. I've had plenty of dream "visits," but so far, not a reading in this format. Watching other people get accurate messages from their loved ones validates for me that Suzanne and Lisa are very close and they know what is happening in my life.

"I want to talk to Roberta," Suzanne Northrup the Medium keeps saying it until I respond. She asks me if I lost a child. "Two" I say. And she says "the letter L" right away. Well that's Lisa. She identifies the "other child" by mentioning a "stuffy," which may seem random, but is not. Suzanne had only one. We called it her "teeny tiny pillow," because it kept losing stuffing. Each time I stitched it up, it became smaller and smaller, until it became an unidentifiable "stuffy thing." The day before I had been thinking about the time when Lisa was born and Suzanne, just over two years old, came to visit me with her dad. She had her Teeny Tiny with her, but she lost it at the hospital and had to go home without it. *How did she sleep that night?* The next day a nurse walked into my room with Teeny Tiny pinned to her uniform, knowing that it had been well-loved by some unknown child.

The medium said that there was a big gap between the losses. True. 17 years! She added that with Suzanne it was a "roller coaster." Also true. She told me that Lisa was right there with us the whole time and that Suzanne "really tried."

Just a brief few minutes of conversation with the girls. It is never enough. I always want more. An exhilirating energy fills me as I bask in the brief moments I can connect in this way.

***

A couple of weeks later I'm having a coffee in Rittenhouse Square. A busker is singing "Harvest Moon," and I am immediately transported to the 90's when I'm driving home from the Four Winds Psychiatric Facility in upstate New York at the end of a September day.

I'm processing my visit with Suzanne. That was when she broke her jaw after "falling" off a roof drunk and we didn't know if it was intentional. Her jaw was wired shut and she could only consume liquids. That day she managed some wonton soup through a straw in a local Chinese place. I was out of my mind trying to figure out what the hell was happening with my daughter. Things were so crazy then.

The light was beginning to shift and I could feel a change in the season, as trees were already turning golden. Driving south on the highway, I witnessed a glorious sunset as the fiery orange-red orb made its way behind the gentle hills.

This was the beginning of the "rehab tour" that would ultimately allow to Suzanne to experience recovery and a brilliant beginning to her college experience.

All that from a song.

What a journey we would have! Lisa was still alive then. In this moment, sitting on a park bench in Philadelphia, nearly 30 years later, I realize that I'm not only remembering the chaos, but also the moments of beauty. I like that.

CHAPTER 64

Making Peace

As Lisa's 21st anniversary approaches, I feel her close. I read a passage in my new Thich Nhat Hanh book titled, "Passing Away Does not Mean Gone." Something clicks. This sounds familiar. I remember that I have written something similar in my earlier book. It came from a dream that I had after Suzanne died, but it is Lisa who speaks, "Passing away is just in the mind." she says in the dream. I am happy to have another reminder that my kids have never left me.

***

I begin to let myself think more about Lisa. Because I have made peace with Suzanne, I can do this. My friend, Maria and I do happy hour at Bar Bon Bon on Lisa's anniversary. Suzanne had taken me there just before she moved to Dallas. "Tell me about Lisa," Maria says. That was the best gift I have ever had on an anniversary. And I tell her all about Lisa. About her sense of humor. Her big heart. How she walked a blind man home after an AA meeting in NYC. And how much she loved living with me there. That night when we walked on the Brooklyn Bridge gazing at the magical city lights, high above the traffic, when she was on top of the world and her whole life was in front of her.

***

Life after the pandemic is coming back. Going out feels safer, but it is still a little scary. I am back to work part time. When I go to the theater I have so many issues with the folding seats. I have forgotten how bags and sweaters can fall into the opening. It is strange to have people sitting so close. I have conversations with random people that I meet in the park. One day I get flustered when a man expresses some interest in dating me and I exit abruptly, leaving behind my bag of apples from the farmers' market. He shouts after me and I have to go back and retrieve it. I host writing group and serve vegetable soup to my new friends on my old kitchen table. My place gets cleaned up. This is the first time I have served a meal in my apartment in years. All of this is good.

But I still have anxiety and afib. The newness of getting out in the world creates another kind of stress. My doc suggests a daily beta-blocker to control the heartbeat, and at first, it seems like a miracle, but it's not a complete cure. Managing my stress continues to be an issue. I keep up with the acupuncture and study the vagus nerve. I try not to overbook myself, or have unrealistic expectations for people, including me.

Sometimes, it is just my own mind that makes everything worse. I practice mindfulness as much as possible.

Six weeks until Iceland. I can't wait.

* * *

Nov. 10, 2021,

Dear Suzanne,

Happy Birthday, Suzanne! I posted your photo on Facebook and you are getting a lot of attention. I wrote that "I miss you in my heart," because it's true. When I release anger, fear, and guilt, there's space for my heart to open to you in the way I've been hoping for. And you have been shining through. I've felt you very close this week.

You might not be surprised that I am taking beta-blockers every day now. You were the one who told me years ago that people take them for anxiety, and now I'm one of them. I've also been doing some vagus nerve yoga and exercises to calm my nervous system. You were the one who always said I had " a vagus nerve thing." What a smart nurse you were! I've gained weight from comfort eating since the 2016 election and an assortment of other fun things like the pandemic and moving grandma, so it's taking me some time to re-wire myself, but I will do it.

In the new space I have in my heart, I feel the best of your glorious energy and it lifts me. You and Lisa- how lucky I was to have had you both. We will be together again one day (not that I'm rushing it).

I love you more than pistachios.

Love, Momsy

The weather switches to dismal as we move deeper into November. I've brought out the warm layers and merino wool socks that I had bought for Morroco and and I will pack for Iceland. My torso and feet are warm, but the wind makes my eyes drip. The season of drippy eyes. And soup.

I stop at La Columbe for a coffee and overhear the baristas talking about chicken and rice. "I ate that for weeks while in Mexico," I pipe in. One barrista shares that he's feeding this bland diet to his dog who has stomach issues. "You don't need anything besides that," he adds and I agree. I suggest making soup and he said he already has.

Chicken and rice and dogs makes me think about my buddy, the resident dog Malo, in Mexico. How he loved the boiled chicken skin. I think about how Suzanne sent the beach dogs to me, but it was clearly the smell of boiling chicken that endeared me to Malo.

***

Another dream…

I am with Ramona in New York City doing all the things she hated in real life— going into museums and walking around. But she was doing them now and it made me feel special.

I have been thinking about Ramona. What a tragic loss of such a deep friendship. In this time of more space, there is time for reflection. I go inward with the season and come to some peace about this loss too.

CHAPTER 65

Not Goodbye

With the gloomy weather, comes shorter days.. We have changed the clocks and the season of early darkness begins, but the biggest darkness is yet to come—Iceland. I will be in the most northern place I have ever been for the shortest, darkest day, where there will be just a few hours of daylight. *What will that feel like?*

It's the weekend before Thanksgiving and the farmers' market has moved to the opposite side of Rittenhouse Square because of the Philadelphia Marathon. I see a couple of runners with space blankets wrapped around their tired bodies and immediately have memories of Suzanne running the race. When I met her at the finish line, she was all glowy and confident. I was impressed and proud of her. I don't know how she did it. We went back to her place for a little celebration and many friends arrived to show their love. I think about her dogs, and how much she loved them. I figured I'd write about tart apples and butternut squash purchased at the market that day, but all I can think about is how much I miss my daughter.

As, Omicron, the next scary variant of the virus, starts making its way around the world, some countries like

Morocco and Israel close their borders. Other countries aren't taking Americans because of our loose vaccine policies. But Iceland is open. With its population 96% fully vaccinated. a test is required before entry.

I get a call from Suzanne's friend, Becca, who invites me to her home to do a version of Cookie Day, with her family. Lauren will also be there. In honor of Suzanne, I want to buy books for her two young boys. The memory is so strong of me reading her books in my lap when she was little. And it's been years since I've bought presents for small children. I go to the kids department at Barnes and Noble, go deep into the vortex of chldren's books, and emerge with the perfect titles.

I'm not dreading the holiday this year. I decorate my window sill with multi-colored mini-lights, shiny balls, and tin angels. I buy some festive holiday paper, ribbon, and tape to wrap up some gifts Mom wants to give to special people at the facility. I wrap the books for Becca's boys. The warm glow in my apartment gives me joy.

I wake up early the next day because I'm thinking about our newly formed writing group. We are having a holiday meal at Marianne's house, just around the corner, and we are all bringing something. I've got the appetizer. Jane will arrive early to help Marianne with the roast. I feel blessed to have this new friend family.

On the way to my last model job before Iceland, I take a meditative walk up St. Martin's Lane from the train station. I am just at the corner where the road bends when I look up and see some antlers. "Oh no, Santa's lost a reindeer," I think. It's a giant stag, majestic in his stance, yet looking a little lost in this manicured garden. He probably wandered out of the Wissahickon's woods in search of food and is as surprised to see me as I am to see him. The closer I get, the more he moves away, crossing the street. Now I am worried that he'll get hit by a car. Luckily, he goes back into the woods. I hoped to see him on the way home but he was long gone, back with Santa where he belongs! I don't take this deer sighting lightly and research the significance of the deer, specifically a stag. I find out that when Deer comes it's a particularly intuitive time. A time to release something that no longer works and make room for the new. I pay close attention to messages that come to me.

I'm ready.

It is just a week before I leave for Iceland and Philadelphia is still golden. From my window I can see a rich display of yellow on an oak on Locust Street The ginko trees that line St. James Place show off their brilliant hues. Every year I wonder why the ginkos hold so tightly to their leaves. Why do they resist moving into hibernation while other trees have lost most of theirs? On most trees, leaves change color, dry up, and fall, but gingo leaves won't wither. Instead, when a cold snap hits, a massive dramatic "drop" of bright golden foliage carpets the street. It's coming. Any day now. I wonder if we all aren't a bit like the ginko — resisting change until we have to.

I find a post on Twitter by @LakotaMan who says that there is no word for goodbye in the Lakota language. Instead they use "Toska," which means "until the heart feels you again." The heart can feel any time, even after a person dies. This connects with the Indigenous concept of no death, "only a change of worlds," as Chief Seattle said. I feel that. We never really "lose" anyone. My girls are always right here; it is up to me to feel them in my heart. And I do. Releasing guilt, has opened my heart and has created more space for sweet memories to enter.

Cookie Day at Craig and Becca's exceeds expectations. Cooper, the older child, is serious, skilled, and disciplined in his creations. He is the one who remembers Aunty Suzanne and might have some questions about her that he never gets to ask. The little one, Henry, is highly focused and gets right onto the table where he finds his own system for cutting out stars in the dough and removing them from the excess. He enjoys creating "abstract art" cookies and drowns them with mountains of sprinkles and other decorative edibles as he vigorously shakes the jars. I may have been more of a task master when my kids were small, but this is the closest I get to grandmother, so I'm much more lenient here. Henry cracks me up. Deep belly laughs evolve into the silent laugh, then tears. What a release.! A little healer that one is! It is so sweet to be with Suzanne's friends. Aunt LaLa (Lauren) is a devoted aunt. They are lucky to have her. I know Aunty Suzanne is right here with us laughing. Lisa too!

CHAPTER 66

Iceland Magic

The absence of light doesn't feel depressing, as one might expect It feels magical. The guide on the Golden Circle Tour says the same thing. It is a special phenomenon that occurs in only a few civilized places. And I have come to experience it! I never feel unsafe walking alone in morning's darkness. Sunrise won't be until around 11:30 AM and all is silent.

On one of my dark morning meanderings, a large black bird, a raven, sits atop a yellow house. I notice him when I stop to take photos of the brightly colored "gingerbread" houses. Hello, Mr. Raven! I walk a bit more and notice him perched on another house—he has been following me! I don't consider this random or coincidental. I believe that this calm bird has come to teach me.

Later I look up the significance of Raven. I discover that Raven represents *change.* If Raven comes into your life, it is encouraging you to bend time and space within your own mind for it to manifest in the physical reality. It also signifies, *rebirth* and *reflection.* Another sign that change is good for me. The idea that changing thoughts alters reality—that's my journey.

I can't explain why I feel so good in Iceland. Is it the clean water, the fresh air, the unhurried, uncrowded city, or the kindness of the people? Maybe it is because I am eating volcanic ash, technically, that is. The lamb, raised only on berries that grow in rich volcanic soil, become the most tender delicacy in winter. The painter/owner of a gallery, a few doors down from the hotel, puts ash in his paintings. He understands the energy it contains.

I think about the journey of Icelandic ash, starting as fire underneath the Earth's surface, so hot that the Earth cannot contain it. It spews from volcanoes eventually ending up in the soil. The energy of fire transforms into food. Nature's wisdom blows my mind.

✳✳✳

I am standing on top of the world, as close to the Arctic Circle as I can get, but I am not alone. Six busloads of Aurora seekers have left Rekyavik, caravan style, for an hour's ride to escape the city lights. We disembark at Thingvellir National Park, while the buses continue to run in case we need to warm up. On a dark, cloudless night, you might see the Northern LIghts, but it is not guaranteed.

I have worn my super warm fur-lined boots, merino wool socks, and a couple of layers, but it is 32 degrees. I don't want to miss a second of the experience. "They just come out of nowhere," the guide tells us. There is an almost full moon in the sky to my right and I wonder if its bright light will

339

affect how we see them. I gaze out straight ahead in the direction that I think they will appear. Orion and the Big and Little Dippers are clearly visible.

At the Aurora Museum the day before, I learned everything I could. The forecast for this night is a "4" which is not 4 out of 10, but rather 40 times more than a 1. There is solar activity, which starts the whole process and is just as important as a cloudless sky. I learned that 4–6 range is perfect for seeing the lights. The solar particles have to find cracks in the Earth's magnetic field, weaker at the poles, in order to dazzle us with a brilliant light show.

After an hour, when my toes start to feel numb, I consider going into the bus for a little warmth. Instead, I jump a little, walk around, and stretch. 30 minutes later, as predicted, a metallic green/white vapor materializes overhead as a bow to my left and then fills up the sky in an arch that covers us. The green rainbow of Aurora Borealis has arrived. Welcome to magnificence! It is so big, I can only photograph it in segments. As I experience the awe of this display, which the sun and the Earth have created, the moon looks on. And again, like in the Sahara, I think of my girls. I know for sure that they are here witnessing this with me. Even when I am alone, I am not alone.

It is in that instance, I feel small, but not in a negative, insignificant way. It is rather that the Universe is so grand and spectacular and I am just a little speck in the scheme of things. Also, I am overcome with a feeling of gratitude for being able to witness the Aurora as it is not guaranteed. In that sense, I feel honored and humbled.

We leave before it is finished and I watch it in the sky from the bus window as we drive away until the lights of the city make it more difficult to see. From a distance it covers a large portion of the sky.

That night I don't sleep much, but enough to have a wonderful dream...

First comes Lisa. I watch her give a speech. Then I sit down on a bench to call Suzanne. Immediately, I hear her voice and look up and she is sitting on a bench directly behind me. She looks beautiful and at peace and we are both so excited to see each other. We decide to go on a city bus and get off at 42nd Street. But, instead we end up in Harlem. We get off and go to the supermarket.

On my last Icelandic night, I dream again of Lisa...

This time she shows up with Scotchy, our family's golden retriever.

I give him a bowl of water which he laps with great pleasure. Lisa and I are supposed to watch a concert together on TV. My friend Lorraine shows up in the dream, with a ticket for me to go with her to a concert. I show Lisa how to work the controls before I leave. I am a little mad that I have to leave Lisa.

Lorraine had come to take me to the land of the living, but I do so knowing my girls are perfect. And so is our dog!

Even though I don't see the sun much on my eight-day trip, on the ride back to the airport I get to study it, as it sets that afternoon. We will have sun for only four hours. Of course it is the Earth on its tilted axis, that is causing this effect. In that moment, I can actually feel the tilt. Our proximity to the Arctic Circle, means that in this season the top of the world is tilted away from the sun, hence the darkness. The exact opposite happens in summer.

We who live in the middle of the poles, experience the four seasons more dramatically and the light more evenly distributed, but rarely see the Aurora. I have never thought so much about the Earth, it's shape and tilt. Such a gift. Such a blessing. Such a validation that there is always more to witness, more than enough reason to continue walking this life with curiousity, awe, and experimentation.

The world is a beautiful place. If I take time to listen to the birds, to study waves, pelicans, or the bark of an ancient sycamore tree, the world expands. Its shape and tilt stays the same, but it is up to me how I perceive and appreciate its gifts and changes.

AFTERWARD

Mother's Day, 2023 (18 Months Later)

I begin the day with a lengthy letter to both my girls. And cover so many topics, but then I address Suzanne specifically…

If we are here in this world to learn from adversity, I have been given a master class. I'm not sure that I would receive a high grade for my performance, but I trudge along. I muddle through as best as I can, continuing to learn new things. I know you see the card playing and the manicures that I do with Grandma and I'm certain that you approve of the new relationship I have with her as she ages. I hope that I honor you as best I can. Because in the end, it is and has always been about love we have for each other. Which never dies.

My heart is open after I write these words and I cry out of love. But I am not done.

I get the urge to go back into Suznne's phone, as I often do, around holidays. It's been a while since I studied photos, emails, and texts looking for answers to the unanswerable question *Why?*

More lately, I have been obsessed with finding the video journal she made of her trek up Kilimanjaro. I had been writing about our travels that week and I was inspired to see what I could do to find them.

They were somewhere on her phone, but she didn't have enough storage, so photos from past years wouldn't load. I had spent hours and hours just deleting stuff with the hopes that one day the videos would have enough room to load themselves (Is that even how it works?) Years ago, I thought I might find some words of wisdom that would answer all my lingering questions. I had let that go. Now I look for happy memories.

I had thought about taking the phone to the Apple Store so one of the geniuses could work on it, but that would involve having to talk about one dead daughter, possibly two, so I always abandoned that idea.

So here I am back to deleting again. On Mother's Day. But something comes to me, not quite a voice, but a powerful extra-strength thought—maybe an angel or God or the Universe or Suzanne.

Forget the phone Get the computer.

Suzanne's computer sits on a high shelf in my walk-in closet. I hadn't looked at it in almost six years. Back then, there was some work stuff and one college essay about when she was happiest in her life. That's all.

This time, I see that essay again and it feels different. It reminds me that there was a time when she had outstanding recovery, a wonderful boyfriend, and was loving college—all before Lisa died. I feel blessed that she had that time, as brief as it was.

Then I notice a folder that I hadn't remembered. And guess what? It's a folder of photos. And yes, the photos from our Africa trip, including the video journal! I scroll down and come upon day three of her five-day trek. Suzanne is at the summit. She describes how hard it is—not the walking, but the wind, and how for seven hours on the final ascent, she was frozen. She adds that she was so happy that her family and friends hadn't climbed with her because they would have been so mad at her. "But here I am, alive," She says this twice with her wind burnt cheeks and her rosy healthy glow and positive attitude that got her to the top of that mountain.

"But here I am, alive." Very much alive in that video. Her energy fills up the room.

My heart is bursting. What a gift on Mother's Day!

I'm so joyous that I have found this and get to see Suzanne, alive and proud of her success. And although there aren't any words that she says that answer any nagging questions, I get that this is the way she wants to be remembered. At the top.

If this book is at all about climbing mountains, this was the easiest kind for Suzanne. The struggles of depression and addiction were harder. We all have our "mountains" to climb.

The relationship that I have with Suzanne now is the best I can have with someone on the Other Side. I continue to reap the benefits of letting go of guilt. More of Suzanne's sweetness and pure soul shines through when I practice grace and self-forgiveness. I knew what I had to do, and when I was ready, I did it.

There are still anxious moments and occasional Afib episodes. More life awaits me, with my angels beside me every step of the way, cheering.

References/ Resources

Grief Support Groups- These are groups that have helped me over the years. They have websites and Facebook groups.

Al-Anon Family Groups (for families/friends of alcoholics) https://al-anon.org/

Alliance of Hope (suicide loss) https://allianceofhope.org/

Compassionate Friends (parents/siblings) https://www.compassionatefriends.org/

Helping Parents Heal http://helptingparentsheal.org/

Tender Hearts (grief support) https://www.davidkesslertraining.com/

Sources

A Year With Hafiz, by Daniel Ladinsky. Penguin Group, New York, 2011.

How to Live When a Loved One Dies, by Thich Nhat Hanh. Edited by Sister Tri Nghie and the editors of Paralex Pres. Berkely, California, 2021.

"Ikkyu, A Renegade Zen Master," by Daniel Scharpenberg. Edited by Dana Gornall, from The Tattooed Buddha website. https://thetattooedbuddha.com/

Pocket Guide to Spirit Animals, by Dr. Steven Farmer. Hay House, Inc, 2012.

The Pocket Pema Chodron, edited by Eden Steinberg. Shambala Publications, Inc., 2000.

Waking up Alive, by Richard A Heckler, Ph.D. Grosset/Putnam, New York, 1994.

What Made Maddy Run, by Kate Fagan. Back Bay Books/ Little Brown and Company/ Hachette Book Group. New York, 2017.

Your Soul's Plan by Robert Schwartz. North Atlantic Books, California, 2009.

Acknowledgments

This book was written over the course of six years and has gone through many drafts and edits.

I have to thank, most of all, Jane Marko, my fearless and constant reader/editor who kept me focused, grounded, and disciplined in the book's final year of revisions. Her friendship and commitment mean more than I have words for.

To my readers Maddy Simon and Sharon Jesser—you gave me just what I needed— honesty, with love.

Thank you also to my memoir/writing gurus. Natalie Goldberg taught me "to go for the jugular" and fill up notebooks with writing practice, which helped me to embellish my story and manage its chronology. Marion Roach Smith, in her excellent courses, helped me create a solid structure for the book.

Honorable mentions go to my favorite writers, Annie Dillard and Mary Karr, who by their examples have set me free.

I am grateful for the support of my writing group— Eleanor, Paula, Marianne, and Jane for creating a safe space to write about anything. Their deep listening has been profound.

And to Mom's Group—Karen, Sharon, Barbara, Toby and Cheryl, who welcomed me, with encouragement, even when I wasn't ready. There was no judgment, only space for listening. These women have provided structure and grounding to get through some of the roughest times and have become so precious to me.

To my friends Bette, Eleanor, Lorraine, and Susan. Your love and support have always carried me through.

And to Suzanne's friends—Lauren, Becca, Nikki, and Devon— thanks for your help with details of past events, and as always, for remembering and loving Suzanne.

And finally, to my daughters—I was blessed to be your mother for as long as I was allowed. A medium once told me that when I was ready to write the books, my girls would help me. Thanks, guys. I feel you here!

About The Author

Roberta Halpern, a former English teacher, left the world of public schools to begin a creative freelance life in 1999. She has been a face painter, a practitioner of Hawaiian massage, a dance program presenter, an artists' model, and an interfaith minister. She lives in Philadelphia where she writes and paints. Her first memoir, *Courage Reborn,* is a handbook for early grief.

You can learn more at her website dragonflyhealingarts.com

Her new blog, A Creative Life, can be found there